an **AMISH PATCHWORK**

Thomas J. Meyers
and
Steven M. Nolt

Indiana's
Old
Orders
in the
Modern
World

an AMISH PATCHWORK

QUARRY BOOKS

AN IMPRINT OF
INDIANA UNIVERSITY PRESS
BLOOMINGTON AND INDIANAPOLIS

A publication of
Quarry Books

an imprint of
Indiana University Press
601 North Morton Street
Bloomington, IN 47404-3797 USA

http://iupress.indiana.edu

Telephone orders   800-842-6796
Fax orders   812-855-7931
Orders by e-mail   iuporder@indiana.edu

The paper used in this publication meets the minimum requirements
of American National Standard for Information Sciences—
Permanence of Paper for Printed Library Materials, ANSI Z39.48-
1984.

Manufactured in the United States of America

Cataloging information is available from the Library of Congress.

ISBN 0-253-34538-3 (alk. paper) — ISBN 0-253-21755-5 (pbk. : alk. paper)

1 2 3 4 5   10 09 08 07 06 05

To Carrie, Rachael, Anicka, Lydia, and Esther

CONTENTS

Illustrations

Acknowledgments

This book draws heavily on interviews, fieldwork, and archival research carried out as part of the "Amish and Old Order Groups of Indiana" project made possible by a grant from the Lilly Endowment, Inc. The project was conducted under the auspices of the Mennonite Historical Library at Goshen College. We are grateful to the Lilly Endowment and to Mennonite Historical Library Director John D. Roth for their support and encouragement. We received helpful guidance during our research from an advisory group that met annually and included John A. Hostetler (1918–2001), Beulah Stauffer Hostetler, Donald B. Kraybill, and four Amish individuals.

During the course of our research we visited every Old Order settlement in Indiana as well as several communities in other states. We are deeply grateful to the dozens of Amish and Old Order Mennonite people who provided us with information and counsel in each place we visited, taking time out of their daily work, visiting with us in their homes, and sharing their ideas and observations. We met many wonderful people and made new friends.

We thank the Lilly Endowment and Goshen College for support in preparing this book manuscript. In addition, we express our gratitude to several Amish readers who critiqued the manuscript as we drafted it. Joel Fath and Dottie Kauffmann provided excellent photo illustrations. Finally, we wish to thank Indiana University Press editorial director Robert J. Sloan for assistance in bringing the volume to publication.

an **AMISH PATCHWORK**

INTRODUCTION
Who Are These People?

In late November 2002, Elkhart County, Indiana, officials attended a ribbon-cutting ceremony for a newly completed stretch of road. Following timeworn tradition, a county commissioner and the county sheriff joined other civic leaders in taking a symbolic first ride down the new road—only this time, they rode in an Amish buggy.

In fact, the new road was a half-mile gravel road accessible only to nonmotorized vehicles and designed to provide Amish travelers with a safer alternative to the busy highway nearby. The road, it turned out, was a joint public-private venture, and the Amish had contributed more than $13,000 toward county construction. The Amish were eager to see the road open since it allowed safer, easier access to one of their most frequent travel destinations: the local Wal-Mart shopping complex.[1]

This story at once confirms and confounds popular stereotypes of the Amish. As expected, the Amish continue to cling to horse-and-buggy travel in the midst of a motorized world, even when preserving this practice demands expensive or innovative alternative means, like a separate road. Yet the road itself—designed to promote their traditional form of transportation—takes its patrons to Wal-Mart, the epitome of modernity's mass-market homogenization and dilution of local community. Clearly, the Amish are living apart from, and yet as a part of, the modern world.

While tourist advertisements, Hollywood movies, and popular fiction have helped promote and reinforce certain Amish images—isolated farms nestled amid neat rows of shocked corn, windmills pumping water for livestock, barefoot children working beside bonneted women and bearded men—these images of bucolic uniformity mask the real diversity that is also part of Amish life and hide the changes that mark these living communities.

On closer inspection, Old Order communities scattered across North America represent remarkable variety, and nowhere is that variety more evident than among Indiana's Old Orders. Different patterns of migration and interaction with outsiders, diverse ethnic customs and folkways, varying economic opportunities and outlets—all shape local Old Order life in particular ways, yet within a framework that is identifiably Amish.

Like a patchwork quilt that combines different colors and shapes with a common thread, Old Order people share important convictions even as they dress differently, take up an assortment of jobs, and maintain their separation from the rest of the world in differing—and changing—ways.

Visible variation is most obvious. For example, while most Indiana Amish buggies are black and are enclosed, others are black but are not enclosed, and riders sit in the open air. Still others are enclosed but gray in color. Similarly, many Amish women's head coverings are white, but some are black, and others are brown.

Other differences are less notable but perhaps more significant. Most Hoosier Amish speak a German dialect known as Pennsylvania Dutch, but others do not. The majority of Amish children attend private Amish schools, but some are enrolled in public schools with non-Amish teachers and classmates. And while some Amish families continue to farm, a growing majority do not—though alternatives to agriculture vary from at-home shops, to work in construction, to industrial factory employment.

Amidst this diversity, however, there are common convictions about faith and family, about the church and its relationship to surrounding society. If the Amish welcome some types of innovation, clearly they resist others, even at great cost. Understanding their beliefs and worldview can help make sense of the myriad differences while revealing the patterns that emerge amid the patchwork pieces. We invite you to examine along with us this Indiana patchwork that sews together remarkable diversity with similar threads.

The chapters that follow present an overview of the central themes and diverse expression of Old Order Amish life in Indiana. The first eight chapters deal exclusively with the Old Order Amish. The ninth chapter, by way of comparison, introduces the Old Order Mennonites, a much smaller group but one with a long history in the Hoosier state. We include the Old Order Mennonites because they are often confused with the Amish in popular images and literature, and we hope to clarify some of that misrepresentation. In addition, we believe this comparison helps to focus some of the issues and themes that shape both groups.

ONE

THE OLD ORDERS
In the World but Not of It

On cold winter mornings all over Indiana, groups of Amish women gather to quilt. Summer work is over, the gardens are clean of all vestiges of summer harvest, and shelves are full of canned fruits and vegetables. Now there is time for neighbors and friends, mothers, sisters, and daughters to work together, piecing material of different colors and shapes into covers that will adorn family beds. Often their handiwork transforms remnants of old sewing projects—the odds and ends of leftover fabric—into beautiful quilts. Although the work is carefully crafted and the stitching is even, the design and color scheme may not be uniform or symmetric.

So it is with the Old Orders themselves. Common convictions and diverse traditions produce a particular pattern from the state's nineteen Old Order Amish and two Old Order Mennonite communities, encompassing more than 35,000 people. Scattered throughout Indiana, Old Orders primarily live in the state's northeastern quadrant but also in east and west central Indiana, and several communities dot the southern portion of the state (table 1.1). Some of these communities are small, with fewer than a hundred people; others include thousands of Old Orders.

Although the variety within these communities is as colorful and varied as a patchwork quilt, we use the common label "Old Order" to name all those who use horse-and-buggy transportation on the road.[1]

The Heart of the Old Order Belief System

Although a surprising degree of diversity characterizes Old Order life, Hoosier Old Orders share many elements of faith and practice with one another—commonalities that connect them and that link them with Old Order groups in other parts of the United States and Canada.[2] Old Order values stand in sharp contrast to those of modern American society. While Americans champion progress or assume that *new* is synonymous with *improved* and that *bigger* equals *better,* Old Orders orient their lives around a different set of assumptions. Understanding these values is essential for making sense of Amish life. Four core beliefs—based on their Christian convictions and reading of the Bible—unite all Old Order groups: (1) the individual finds meaning only in the community of believers; (2) there must be a clear and visible distinction between that church community and the larger society ("the world"); (3) church members should rely primarily on one another and not on institutions of the larger society for support; and (4) the wisdom of tradition is most often a better guide for living life than is the inherently uncertain promises of innovation and change.

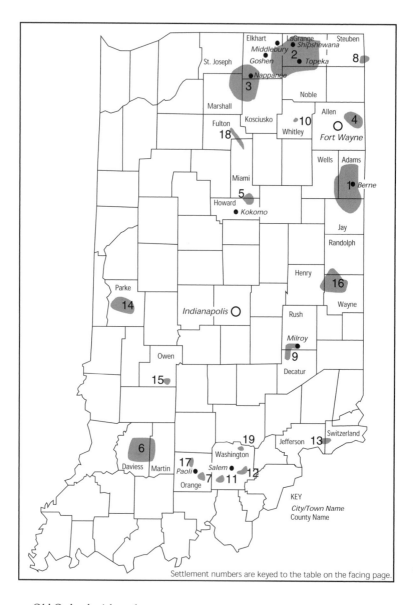

Old Order Amish settlements. MAP BY LINDA EBERLY.

Table 1.1. Old Order Amish Settlements in Indiana

Settlement	Origin	Size in 2002
1. Berne (Adams-Jay-Wells Counties)	1840	32 church districts
2. Elkhart-LaGrange (Elkhart-LaGrange-Noble Counties)	1841	114 church districts
3. Nappanee (Marshall-Kosciusko-St. Joseph-Elkhart Counties)	1842	33 church districts
4. Allen County	1844	14 church districts
5. Kokomo (Howard-Miami Counties)	1848	2 church districts
6. Daviess-Martin Counties	1868	19 church districts
7. Paoli (Orange County)	1957	2 church districts
8. Steuben County, Ind./Williams County, Ohio	1964	2 church districts
9. Milroy (Rush-Decatur Counties)	1970	4 church districts
10. South Whitley (Whitley County)	1971	1 church district
11. Salem (Washington County)	1972	1 church district
12. Salem (Washington County)	1981	2 church districts
13. Vevay (Switzerland-Jefferson Counties)	1986	2 church districts
14. Parke County	1991	4 church districts
15. Worthington (Owen-Greene Counties)	1992	1 church district
16. Wayne-Randolph-Henry Counties	1994	3 church districts
17. Paoli (Orange-Lawrence Counties)	1994	1 church district
18. Rochester (Fulton-Miami Counties)	1996	1 church district
19. Vallonia (Washington-Jackson Counties)	1996	1 church district

A traditional Amish farm, east of Goshen, typifies the rural lifestyle popularly associated with the Amish. Although most Amish continue to live in rural areas, today only a minority is engaged in farming.
PHOTO BY DENNIS L. HUGHES.

The Individual and Society

"While Moderns are preoccupied with 'finding themselves,'" sociologist Donald Kraybill has noted, "the Amish are engaged in 'losing themselves.'"[3] In sharp contrast to the dominant culture of the United States, which exalts the individual, the Amish believe that in losing their individual identities they will find a stronger identity in their collective community of faith. Based on their understanding of Christian humility, the Amish believe that personal ambitions are secondary to Holy Scriptures, centuries of church tradition, and family obligations. Indeed, the ideal relationship between individual Old

Order believers and their community can be described with the German word *Gelassenheit,* which means submission—to God, to others, and to the church.[4] Submission allows the collective wisdom and prudence of the community to govern the priorities of the individual.

Gelassenheit affects nearly every facet of Amish behavior and relationships, from the plain style of clothing and reluctance to pose for photographs, to the general hesitancy to sign their names to public documents or to be quoted by name in the newspaper. When it is time for the all-church noon meal following Sunday morning worship, men and women quietly whisper, "You go first. No, you," as each seeks to be the last one seated. Gelassenheit suggests that the volume of one's voice should rarely be raised and that one show deference to others by remaining silent in a moment of uncertainty before replying to a question.

Gelassenheit also assumes that a humble demeanor is far more appropriate than arrogance or pride. Thus an Amish minister will nearly always begin his sermon with a comment about how unworthy he is to preach, and he will ask his flock to bear with him patiently. He will end the sermon by asking fellow ministers to give testimony, inviting them to "please correct what I have said incorrectly" or to add insights of their own. This simple request for correction and embellishment is a regular reminder that no individual has the last word before the body of believers.

Within the family, Gelassenheit emerges in a primary disciplinary task of parents who seek to "break the will of the child" in order to promote a sense of collective consciousness in place of individual willfulness. As soon as children are self-aware, they must learn to respect the tradition of parents and understand what it will mean if they should decide to join the church as adults. Membership requires submission to an authority beyond the self.

Gelassenheit is also directly tied to simplicity. An Amish home is to be furnished modestly. Any ostentation or unnecessary decorations suggest that the homeowner is trying to gain attention. Although some settlements allow upholstered furniture, none permit wall-to-wall carpeting, the display of human portraits, or full-length mirrors.

Symbolic Separation

When a car whizzes past a horse and buggy slowly making its way to town, the car itself reminds the occupants of the buggy of the divide between the assumptions and values of mainstream culture and their own Amish counterculture. The plain people consider this boundary between themselves and the rest of the world to be a vital part of their faith and community. "Worldliness" is a sign that the boundary is breaking down; giving in to the habits of the world is, in a real sense, giving in to evil. Many elements of Amish culture that outsiders find so outmoded are symbols of that separation and help make the boundaries between the Amish and non-Amish worlds unmistakably clear. Thus the use of horse-and-buggy transportation, the wearing of bonnets and beards, the houses with no electricity from public power lines—all are tangible indicators that the Amish are different from their neighbors. In some cases, of course, the differences are more than symbolic: Old Order choices also fundamentally shape life in important ways. But symbolic or substantive, Old Order separation from the world is real.

An Amish woman shopping at a Wal-Mart Super Center near Goshen loads her purchases into a cargo van driven by a non-Amish driver who brought her to town. Cash income from nonfarm occupations and the presence of suburban retail stores has changed some Amish purchasing patterns in this relatively progressive Amish settlement.
PHOTO BY JOEL FATH.

The Amish are keenly aware of this distinction between "the world," which includes a great deal of evil, and the church and all that is good. They accept literally the biblical injunction of Romans 12:2 that Christians should conform, not to the standards of this world, but to a higher calling of God. Part of that calling is commitment to a community of believers—the royal priesthood mentioned in 1 Peter 2:9 or the "peculiar people" cited in Titus 2:11–14.

In contrast, the Amish generally use "the world" to describe everyone and everything that stands apart from their under-

The Amish settlement just east of Paoli is remarkably conservative, and houses are notably austere inside and out. Here windmills are still the means of drawing water, and homes have none of the landscaping or patio decks that might be found in more progressive settlements. PHOTO BY THOMAS J. MEYERS.

standing of the gospel. For example, to be "worldly" is to live a way of life that follows the latest fashions, aspires toward professionalism, becomes computer literate, spends a lot of money and time on leisure activities, and assumes that televisions and DVD players are necessities.

It is particularly important to the Amish that the boundary between church and state is clear. Although they believe that a corrupt world requires human government, including a military and a police force to provide order, the Amish avoid involvement in anything that places them in direct contact with government. They refuse participation in the military, and most do not accept Social Security payments or other forms of government subsidy.

The Church as Regulator and Sustainer

The Old Order Amish church wields a great deal of influence over individual members, but along with limited personal freedom comes the joyful support and security of the church community. Joining the church requires submission to authority. Every local congregation—or "church district," as the Amish call them—has its own *Ordnung*, or set of prescribed guidelines for living. Yielding to the Ordnung is understood to be acting like Christ, who willingly submitted to the will of God, even to the point of his own death.

While the Old Order Amish recognize the Bible as the ultimate source of authority, only through the community of believers can the Bible rightly be interpreted and its power exercised. The community reaffirms its understanding of faithful living twice a year during a church service devoted to a discussion of the Ordnung and known as the "Ordnung's Gemee" (*Gemee*, the Pennsylvania Dutch word for church, can also be used to describe a church service). This preparatory service, which is held two weeks prior to communion, is a solemn occasion where together church members review the common understandings that guide community life and reconfirm their commitment to living in accordance with them.

The ultimate sanction of the church is its power to expel a member. For Old Orders, to be separated from the church is to be thrust into the world, with all of its vices and temptations. On the rare occasion when an individual is unrepentant and continues willfully to disobey the church, he or she may be excommunicated—or, as the Amish say, "placed under the ban." In most communities such an individual then will be "shunned"; that is, church members will avoid unrepentant individuals in certain symbolic ways, such as not sharing a meal or entering into business relationships with them, in order to remind both parties of the broken baptismal vow standing between them. Shunning is a matter the Amish take seriously, but it is a rare occurrence and is practiced more strictly in some places than others.

The other side of church discipline is accountability and commitment. Members know and support one another and live by an ethic of mutual aid. The church is not an abstraction but a living, breathing social body. It is that group of people that an Old Order individual knows he or she can depend on in a time of need and to which each person expects to contribute some form of assistance.

The Old Orders assist members from the cradle to the grave. When a new baby is born, relatives and neighbors come into the home and help the new mother with household responsibilities. If a fire destroys a house or barn, the grieving family can count on an outpouring of financial and emotional support from the community while recovering from the loss and rebuilding the structure. The vast majority of the Amish do not purchase commercial health insurance because they believe that the sick should depend on the church rather than on a worldly institution in times of need. At the end of life the church also provides assistance to the grieving family by taking over farm and home chores; arranging church benches for the funeral service, which takes place in the home; constructing or obtaining the traditional coffin; and seeing that the grave is dug.

Tradition

On Sunday mornings near Nappanee, Indiana, in the midst of the three-hour church services that mark biweekly worship in each Amish church district, men and women rise from their church benches as the minister reads aloud the Scripture passages for the day. But while the men face the assembled ministers, the women stand with their backs toward them. If a curious visitor asks how or why this particular ritual began, the Amish will say that they do not know, but their grandmothers and grandfathers before them also stood and turned accordingly. Continuing this tradition—even if they do not know its origin—symbolizes their fidelity to other forms of authority, including the Scripture being read.

In a world that prizes progress and change, Old Order groups tenaciously hold on to tradition. Tradition is a secure source of authority, drawing on the wisdom of past generations and anchoring life in tried and trusted principles. While many Amish traditions are rooted in biblical commands, others are simply proven or prudent practices that give meaningful shape to a shared life. "It's the way we've always done things," they might explain. Convention is valued more than innovation because it has endured through time and is not as susceptible to the whims of popular culture.

So while North Americans assume that progress is positive, the Old Orders view stability as desirable. Rather than adopting the latest fashions and newest technological options—buying cappuccinos, laptop computers, Nintendo games, SUVs, and digital cameras—they believe that gradual and deliberate change is the preferable way of coping with the unknowns that innovation inevitably brings.

Most Old Order Amish have a keen sense of their own family history. Many know the names of their ancestors going back several generations and are quite familiar with the persecution of their people in the sixteenth century. Along with the Bible

This Amish home in the relatively progressive Milroy, Indiana, Old Order settlement may not be immediately identifiable as Amish-owned. Its appearance contrasts sharply with that on page 12.
PHOTO BY THOMAS J. MEYERS.

and a modest assortment of church publications, Amish homes often have a copy of *The Martyrs' Mirror,* a thousand-page volume detailing stories of forebears who died for their faith.[5]

One of the most remarkable examples of the Amish adherence to tradition is the music they use in worship. Their hymnal, the *Ausbund,* includes sixteenth-century martyr ballads that recount the suffering of their spiritual ancestors as well as hymns written by prisoners awaiting execution because of their faith.[6] To twenty-first-century ears, these songs sound like funeral dirges because of their slow cadence and soulful quality. Indeed, some communities take more than twenty minutes to sing just four verses of a single hymn. Leery of the speed at which the world operates, the Amish label modern gospel songs with quick tempos—like those Amish young people occasionally sing at evening gatherings—"fast tunes," and they do not permit such songs in their regular morning worship.

Other Clues to Commonality

All Old Order Amish also share an inclination for small-scale, face-to-face organizations. Their churches and communities are not highly bureaucratized. Indeed, they have no formal structure beyond the local congregation—no denominational headquarters, no conferences or synods, no sponsored institutions. Yet Amish society is organized in particular ways, and understanding those patterns helps make sense of the choices and practices, and even of the variety that flourishes among them.

Three terms that are important for understanding Amish society are district, settlement, and affiliation. Local Amish churches are known as *districts,* or church districts. The Amish see church as people rather than property, and so do not worship in church buildings. Instead, they meet in members' homes, rotating the hosting of church services from one household to another. To better facilitate this rotation, church districts are defined geographically, with all those living in a given area comprising a given district. When the membership of a district grows too large to meet comfortably in one place, the district divides—again, along geographic lines. As a result, Amish church districts all include roughly the same number of people—there are no Amish "megachurches"—which adds to the homogeneity of Amish life and helps maintain some

Members of the Amish settlement southwest of Salem hold their bi-weekly Sunday morning worship in this meetinghouse, built in 1979, and are the only Amish in the state with this sort of established worship space. All other Amish rotate the hosting of worship services from household to household, holding church in houses, barns, or other private structures. PHOTO BY THOMAS J. MEYERS.

churchly equilibrium in Amish communities. In 2002 Elkhart-LaGrange settlement church districts each included on average 139 people—65 adult members and 74 children and unbaptized teens.[7] In communities where the typical house size is a bit larger or smaller, the average number of people per district may vary accordingly.

Each district has its own ordained leadership, which almost always consists of a bishop, two ministers, and a deacon. The bishop oversees church life and guides congregational decision making in addition to carrying out the ritual responsibilities of preaching, baptizing, and conducting weddings and funerals.

Ministers assist the bishop, whereas deacons tend to the physical needs of members, coordinate mutual aid, and help with matters of church discipline. Leaders serve without salary or specialized higher education. A man's commitments to the church and to modeling a disciplined life—not his speaking ability or his individual sense of calling—are the most important credentials.

A *settlement* is a group of Amish church districts in a given geographic area that also share a common history. Some, like the Elkhart-LaGrange settlement that in 2002 included 114 districts in three contiguous counties, are quite large. Other settlements are small and have only a single district. Settlements may be geographically adjacent, as are the two near the southern Indiana town of Paoli, but they are still considered distinct settlements because each has a different origin and history.

Amish church districts that recognize one another's discipline constitute an *affiliation*. The Amish themselves often use the language of "fellowship," indicating, for example, that they are "in fellowship" with certain other districts. Among other things, churches of a common affiliation allow their bishops and ministers to preach in one another's worship services. Some affiliations are closely delineated, and all parties know where the boundaries of fellowship stop. In other cases the borders are a bit more blurred. An affiliation is different from a settlement. In some cases all the districts in a given settlement comprise a common affiliation, while in other places a settlement may include several different nonfellowshipping affiliations. Affiliations are not limited by geography, and some include districts from a number of settlements.

Common Threads

Core convictions regarding community, separation, discipline, and tradition unite the Old Order Amish throughout Indiana and across North America, where they live in twenty-eight states and the Canadian province of Ontario. These convictions shape Amish life in unmistakable ways, setting them apart from the modern mainstream. They also support the Amish interest in local, tradition-guided organization and authority, which has in turn spawned a good deal of diversity in local custom, practice, and interpretation.

In fact, these common convictional threads that stitch together the Old Order patchwork make possible—even encourage—the variety within the patchwork pattern of Old Order life itself. Differences in migration streams, ethnic traditions, and church discipline color the contemporary quilt of Amish life as do the textures of surrounding neighbors and local economic opportunity. Despite its real diversity, this array of histories, customs, and contemporary environments forms a fabric of fundamental unity and beauty that is Amish society.

The Larger Amish and Mennonite "Family"

Amish groups	Mennonite groups
Old Order Amish	Old Order Mennonites
New Order Amish	"Wisler" Mennonites
Beachy Amish/Amish Mennonite	Conservative Mennonite Conference
	Mennonite Church USA

If the Old Order Amish are the best-known members of their spiritual family tree, they are not without religious cousins in Indiana. Both Amish and Mennonites trace their origins to the sixteenth-century Protestant Reformation. One leader within that movement was a Dutch reformer named Menno Simons. His leadership resulted in the nickname given to the churches he led: *Mennonites*. Later, in 1693, the fellowship experienced a painful division, out of which a distinct group under the leadership of Jakob Ammann came to be known as *Amish* (chapter 2 describes these events in more detail). Both groups immigrated to North America and over time formed a variety of groups reflecting the many ways they have sought to put their beliefs into practice.

To the casual observer, the horse-and-buggy-driving *Old Order Mennonites* are easily confused with the Amish. Old Order Mennonites live notably simple lives, sharing Amish misgivings about the utility and desirability of modern notions of progress and individualism. Chapter 9 describes the Old Order Mennonites in more detail.

The so-called *Wisler Mennonites* are related to the Old Orders but are less conservative in lifestyle and appearance. For example, they drive dark-colored cars rather than buggies. They use English in their worship services but share some common convictions with Old Orders regarding worship and other practices.

Members of the *Conservative Mennonite Conference* seek to uphold certain traditional doctrinal emphases but are much more engaged with the wider world than are the Old Orders, including involvement in a wide range of occupations, active mission work, and some forms of higher education. While some women wear small head coverings, men are indistinguishable from non-Mennonites.

The largest and also most progressive wing of the Mennonite family in Indiana is known as *Mennonite Church USA*. It sponsors a range of institutions, from colleges and seminaries to retirement homes and mental health care centers. Its members are often highly engaged with the wider society, whether through professional pursuits or through mission and service work.

Groups that today identify themselves as Amish include not only the Old Orders but also the so-called New Order Amish and the Beachy Amish (or Amish Mennonites). The *New Order Amish* share much with their Old Order Amish religious kin, including horse-and-buggy culture and identifiably traditional dress patterns, but the New Orders employ a more explicit language of personal salvation and are also somewhat less wary of technology—for example, permitting telephones in homes. The *Beachy Amish* (or Amish Mennonites) are plain in their appearance but clearly less traditional than Old Orders in lifestyle. Beachy Amish members drive cars, use English in worship, and place emphasis on evangelism and missions. More information about both the New Order Amish and the Beachy Amish is included in chapter 3.

TWO

MOVING TO INDIANA

T he Amish have always been a people on the move. If popular images associate the Amish with stubbornly enduring communities that persist for generations, the Amish themselves are apt to know that migration has been a central theme in a story of a people who consider themselves among the biblical "strangers and pilgrims" in a foreign land.

From their late-seventeenth-century beginnings in Switzerland and the Palatinate to their arrival in North America and movement across the continent, the Amish have never been hesitant to move, even when transportation was limited to horses or railroads. During the last century and a half, scores of Amish settlements have taken root across the United States— and dozens more have come to an end, their members scattering for any number of reasons, some to move back to older settlements and others to launch new communities somewhere else.[1] Although migration still demands significant time, planning, and energy, it remains a significant part of Indiana Amish life. Six of the state's nineteen settlements have begun since 1991, with the majority of the newcomers arriving from Pennsylvania, Ohio, and New York.

Some Amish do spend their lives in one area—perhaps even on the same farm, surrounded by familiar neighbors and kin. But if deep roots in a family farmstead is common, so too is the Amish person who was born in one settlement, later lived in another state, and eventually died in yet a third location. Old Order identity is connected to a sense of peoplehood and community that transcends any specific piece of land. Both their religious rootedness and their history of migration are part of the fabric of the Indiana patchwork.

Anabaptist Roots

The Amish story is rooted in the memory of the Protestant Reformation of the 1500s. During these years, as mainstream Reformers like Martin Luther, John Calvin, and Ulrich Zwingli challenged some of the teachings of the late medieval Catholic Church, small groups of religious radicals in cities and rural areas of Switzerland, south Germany, and the Netherlands offered a more thoroughgoing critique. They insisted that the Christian church had a purpose and orientation clearly different from that of larger society, and they called for a sharp separation of the "kingdom of God" from the "kingdom of the world."[2]

For these radicals the church was properly composed only of those who had made the voluntary—and often costly—decision to set themselves apart from evil and follow the teaching of Jesus. A state church that equated membership with citizenship, or baptized all infants as a matter of course, had no basis in

Scripture, they insisted. Instead, they understood baptism as a sign of one's conscious choice to join the church—a choice reserved for adults aware of the implications of Christian discipleship. Since years earlier these radicals themselves had been baptized as infants in the state church, they rebaptized each other. Civil authorities regarded their new adult baptisms as illegal and condemned the radicals as *Anabaptists* (meaning rebaptizers). A loosely organized movement, Anabaptism had no single or central leader, though in some places, using the name of an influential Dutch Anabaptist leader named Menno Simons, people nicknamed them Mennists (or Mennonites).

Most Anabaptists were orthodox Christians, grounding their faith in the Bible and in traditional doctrines of the Trinity, human sin, and God's grace. But they also advocated several specific interpretations of faith that distinguished them. Their understanding of the church as a primary and alternative community, distinctly different from the state, undercut the notion of a unified society in which church and state had similar goals. The Anabaptists insisted that Christians should practice the teachings of Jesus Christ in all of life's daily activities, thus rejecting participation in the military, self-defense, or other sorts of violence. Some Anabaptist groups held to radical economic practices based on the teachings of the early church recorded in Acts 2 and 4 in which members of the community held all of their property in common. And most Anabaptists refused to swear oaths and discouraged luxury and fancy dress.

All of these practices put them at odds with both mainstream religious leaders and political authorities. Condemned as dangerous heretics and subversive of the civic order, the Anabaptists found themselves harassed, jailed, and in some

In 1571 authorities in Amsterdam executed Anneken Hendriks for her Anabaptist beliefs. Her story is included in *Martyrs' Mirror,* a lengthy volume of Anabaptist accounts still read by the Amish today. ETCHING COURTESY MENNONITE HISTORICAL LIBRARY, GOSHEN, IND.

cases executed. Between 1527 and 1614 some four thousand were martyred.

Mennonites and Amish

Central to the Anabaptist understanding of Christian faithfulness was the conviction that one's beliefs must be closely connected with daily life. For them, right living was as important as right thinking. This central orientation also proved to be the source of periodic conflict in Anabaptist circles as members debated the practical implications of practicing their faith. In some ways these questions were easier to answer when the Anabaptists faced outright persecution. The lines separating the Anabaptists from the world were relatively clear when the rest of the world wanted no part of them.

But violent opposition to the Anabaptists eventually came to an end. To be sure, some legal discrimination continued, but by the late 1600s hostility against the Anabaptists had generally given way to grudging respect and even quiet admiration for these people who took ethics seriously and withstood the pressure of social ostracism. For the Anabaptists, however, this new acceptance posed a novel problem. How should a people whose identity was based on separation from the world live when the world suddenly seemed ready to tolerate them?

Particularly in Switzerland, the Anabaptists debated this question and found little consensus. Some saw the possibility of social acceptance as a welcome window of relief for which they had long hoped. Others believed that such openness brought a dangerous temptation to compromise their faith and lose sight of their primary loyalty to Christ. Would friendship with the world tempt them to forget the seriousness of discipleship?

In 1693 this discussion took on new urgency when a junior Anabaptist minister named Jakob Ammann pressed a senior leader named Hans Reist to talk about controversial issues within the church. Ammann served a group of congregations in Alsace, where opposition to Anabaptists was relatively light. Reist, by contrast, lived in the old Swiss Anabaptist community where persecution had been harsh and any form of social acceptance of the Anabaptists seemed like a breath of fresh air.[3]

One of the issues the two debated was church discipline.

Ausbund

das ist:

Etliche schöne

Christliche Lieder,

Wie sie in dem Gefängnis zu Passau in dem
Schloß von den Schweizer=Brüdern und
von anderen rechtgläubigen Christen
hin und her gedichtet worden.

Allen und jeden Christen,

Welcher Religion sie seien, unpartheiisch sehr
nützlich.

Nebst einem Anhang von sechs Liedern.

---

13. Auflage.

Verlag von den Amischen Gemeinden
in Lancaster County, Pa.
1980.

The *Ausbund* contains sixteenth-century martyr ballads and other
hymns that tie Amish worship to its Reformation roots. First published
in 1564, it is still used on Sunday mornings by nearly all Indiana Amish.
The Amish in the Daviess County settlement sing from a variation of
the *Ausbund* known as *Unparteiische Liedersammlung.* IMAGE COURTESY
MENNONITE HISTORICAL LIBRARY, GOSHEN, IND.

Ammann argued that because church membership had important social dimensions, breaking with the church also had social implications. If the church was a real community and not just a collection of individuals, then those who willingly and unrepentantly broke their baptismal vows were also severing other relationships. Faithful church members needed to avoid, or shun, the unrepentant in certain ways, such as not eating at the same table or entering into business contracts with them. This symbolic avoidance, known as shunning, disrupted ordinary relationships and reminded everyone of the broken spiritual relationship that stood between them. Ammann insisted that the New Testament taught social avoidance and pointed out that it was part of several early Anabaptists' confessions of faith.

For his part, Reist was ready to allow a more flexible approach to church discipline. He thought shunning was too harsh and was perhaps even vindictive. Reist challenged Ammann to show more grace and forbearance with the wayward. Ammann responded that shunning was the loving thing to do since it demonstrated the seriousness of the situation and was intended to help the person see the error of his or her way, rather than to punish. Indeed, discipline was a form of grace, Ammann insisted, since repentance and restoration to the community was always possible.

When Reist refused to respond to Ammann's summons to a conversation, Ammann and his supporters announced that a formal split had divided the Anabaptist community. Though Ammann's party later showed some interest in healing the rift, Reist's group was not interested. Ammann's supporters eventually came to be known as the *Amish*. In North America Reist's tradition became associated with the Anabaptist label *Mennonite*.

In the early 1700s both the Amish and Mennonites were attracted by the offer of religious freedom and available land in the Quaker colony of Pennsylvania and responded by immigrating to North America.[4] There the Amish and Mennonites remained distinct groups, marked by differences in church discipline and by greater vigilance among the Amish in maintaining separation from the world. Nevertheless, some of the tensions between the two groups lessened, and their shared Anabaptist beliefs and practices gave them a sense of commonality in an American society marked by religious diversity.

Paths to Indiana

One way to make sense of the patchwork nature of today's Indiana Amish communities is to think about when, why, and how they came to live here. Amish arrived in North America from Europe in several distinct waves.[5] From the 1730s to 1770s some three hundred Amish immigrated to Pennsylvania, a small part of a much larger movement of German-speaking peoples who made their way to North America during those same years. These Amish families settled amid other Pennsylvania German households—Lutheran, Reformed, and Moravian folks, for the most part—and their descendants still populate the old Amish settlements in Pennsylvania's Lancaster, Mifflin, and Somerset Counties.

Not all the heirs of those eighteenth-century arrivals remained in the east, however. In 1840, attuned to the popular prospect of westward migration, four Amish men from southwestern Pennsylvania arrived in Indiana to scout land for a new settlement. Given the difficulties of land transportation at the time, the men had first traveled by boat down the Ohio River, then up the Mississippi River to Burlington, Iowa, where they set out on foot to explore farming possibilities in eastern Iowa. Though they were impressed with what they saw, they decided to explore northern Indiana as well. After walking across northern Illinois to Chicago, they took a boat across Lake Michigan and up the St. Joseph River to the Elkhart County village of Goshen.

As one of the men's sons later reported, "When the other Brothers and Sisters [in the church in Somerset County, Pennsylvania] heard the good news from the land seekers, that these explorers had seen a good and flourishing region and well-contented settlers in Indiana, many of them became interested in emigrating westward."[6] The next year four households took up farms east of Goshen. Soon joined by other Pennsylvania and Ohio Amish, they formed what would eventually become the Elkhart-LaGrange settlement, the largest Amish community in the state.

A similar story of westward movement unfolded in 1848 as Amish families from Ohio's Holmes and Tuscarawas Counties moved to the area just east of Kokomo, Indiana. The Hochstetler, Gerber, and Schrock families in this migration were descendants of eighteenth-century immigrants to Pennsylvania who had moved to Ohio.

In contrast, a *second wave* of Amish emigrants from Europe, arriving roughly from 1815 to 1860, largely bypassed Pennsylvania and settled directly in the Midwest. Though they shared the same Amish faith, they often discovered a significant cultural gap between themselves and the heirs of the eighteenth-century arrivals who had almost a century of American experience under their belts. European Amish with roots in Switzerland were part of this later wave of immigration, and

In about 1844, European-born Amish immigrants Henry Stahly
(1810–1894) and Magdalena Ehrisman Stahly (ca. 1812–1879) settled
on land that later became the town of Nappanee. PHOTO CA. 1875,
COURTESY JOHN STAHLY.

they settled in eastern Indiana's Allen and Adams Counties, giving these settlements a distinctly different cultural cast.[7]

In at least one Indiana community, Amish from both of these immigration streams settled together. In 1842 recently arrived European immigrants Christian Stahly (1820–1909) and Veronica Housour Stahly (1822–1897) took steps to purchase land near what would later become the northern Indiana town of Nappanee. Christian was soon joined by several of his brothers, their widowed mother, and other recent Amish immigrants such as the Ringenberg and Berlincourt families. In short order, however, the area also became home to Amish families stemming from first-wave immigrants to Pennsylvania—households bearing names like Yoder, Hochstetler, and Miller. Eventually the Old Order Amish church that developed around Nappanee was composed largely of first-wave descendants, while the Stahlys and their second-wave compatriots affiliated with Mennonite churches.

Migration Continues

Amish settlement in Indiana did not end with the 1840s and 1850s establishment of the communities in northern Indiana, eastern Allen and Adams Counties, and Kokomo. From time to time Amish families continued to leave established homes and form new settlements elsewhere in the state, adding to the variety of places Hoosier Amish called home. In many cases the new settlements retained informal ties to older communities through frequent visiting and the exchange of ministers for church services. Newer settlements often continued the same Ordnung (church and lifestyle patterns) as that observed in the churches from which the first settlers came. For example, new settlements stemming from the Adams County community, such as those near Salem or Vevay, use the same style of buggy as the Adams County Amish and maintain other similar customs.[8]

One of the first settlements resulting from migration within Indiana was the Daviess County Amish community in the southwestern part of the state.[9] Beginning in 1869, some nineteen Amish families—many of them part of an extended Graber clan—moved from Allen County to Daviess County. Though they were later joined by households from Ohio, Ontario, and Missouri, the settlement's primary relationship—maintained to the present—was with the Allen County Amish, though over time the Daviess churches developed a church Ordnung somewhat different from that in Allen.

Today the Amish continue to establish new settlements.[10] Some spring from the desire for more farmland, though this is less of a factor in recent years as farming has declined among the Amish. Still, the search for more rural and less congested locations led some families to new areas such as South Whitley and Vallonia. In a few cases, church conflicts in older settlements have birthed new communities as Amish families chose to move away from tense disagreements rather than remain and possibly provoke a schism.

Certainly, not all new settlements spring up within the boundaries of the state. In the late 1800s Amish from the Daviess, Elkhart-Lagrange, and Nappanee settlements were instrumental in establishing a community in North Dakota, which—while it lasted—attracted families from other places too. In 1895 noted northern Indiana Amish church leader Eli J. Bontrager (1868–1958) was among those who moved to North Dakota. Remaining fifteen years, Bontrager took his family to another new community in Wisconsin in 1910, only to return permanently to his native Shipshewana in 1916.[11]

In recent years Indiana Amish households have also founded numerous settlements in other states, launching them for a variety of reasons and often attracting Old Orders with similar backgrounds and convictions. Examples include the Allen County families who started new settlements in Michigan in the 1950s and 1970s, and the Adams County Amish who moved to Seymour, Missouri, in 1968, beginning a community that has continued to grow while retaining its ties to Indiana.

Meanwhile, some northern Indiana Amish of a more traditional bent have moved to Hillsboro, Wisconsin. The settlement formed there in 1985 is generally more conservative in outlook than the Elkhart-LaGrange and Nappanee communities. Likewise, Amish with an interest in a somewhat more evangelical approach to faith have established new communities attracting people with similar sentiments. The Rosebush, Michigan (1981), and Libby, Montana (1992), settlements are among those that have drawn some of these Indiana Amish families.

Recent Arrivals from Other States

Still other Amish settlements in Indiana have resulted from immigration to the state by Amish from other parts of the country. These new settlements are located in rural areas where the newcomers find land that is cheaper or less residentially developed than the areas from which they have come.

Two of these Amish settlements have roots in the large Amish community in Lancaster, Pennsylvania. Desiring less

During the 1990s Amish from Pennsylvania began settling in Parke and Wayne Counties, and their customs, folkways, and surnames mark them as different from Indiana's historic Amish populations. Stoltzfus is a common Amish name in Lancaster, Pennsylvania, but is rare in Indiana outside of these communities composed of recent Pennsylvania migrants.
PHOTO BY STEVEN M. NOLT.

expensive farmland and the dynamics of a smaller settlement, Amish families from Lancaster began moving to Parke County in late 1991 and to Wayne County in 1994. In both cases the migration was a final step in a carefully planned process that involved "land shopping" with real estate agents, contacts with local banks and businesses, and attention to soil quality and weather patterns. These daughter settlements are distinct from other Indiana Amish communities in a number of ways. Visually, the Amish in Parke and Wayne Counties stand out, with their use of gray Lancaster-style buggies as opposed to the

During the 1990s members of the ultra-conservative Swartzentruber Amish affiliation from Ohio and New York established a settlement north of Paoli, Indiana. Their houses and farm buildings reflect a distinctive Ohio Swartzentruber architectural style. PHOTO BY THOMAS J. MEYERS.

black color and style seen elsewhere in the state. Mailboxes reveal common Lancaster surnames such as Fisher, King, Zook, Stoltzfus, or Beiler—names rarely found in other Midwestern Amish communities. Relationships with Pennsylvania remain strong, and trips to Lancaster for weddings, funerals, and general visiting are much more frequent than visits to other, geographically closer Indiana Amish settlements.

Another recent settlement with origins outside of Indiana began in 1994 when members of the Swartzentruber Amish affiliation moved from New York and Ohio to Orange County, settling near the town of Paoli and close to a small, older Amish settlement already in the area. An especially conservative and tradition-minded group, the Swartzentruber affiliation is centered in Wayne County, Ohio, and has daughter settlements in several other states. Swartzentruber homes often replicate the large farmhouse style of eastern Ohio, and their patterns of dress and buggies also mirror Swartzentruber tradition, making them visually distinct from other Indiana Amish groups.

A final cluster of recent arrivals lives in Indiana's so-called New Order Amish settlements. In 1992, responding to a request from a Worthington, Indiana, resident who expressed interest in joining the Amish church, a number of New Order Amish from Belle Center, Ohio, moved to Worthington and formed the nucleus of a new community. That church district—along with one near Salem that is composed of people from various places and backgrounds—comprise Indiana's small New Order affiliation. Relative newcomers to Indiana, the Worthington and Salem Amish maintain primary ties with a network of New Order Amish churches in other states, mostly in Ohio. (More details about the New Order affiliation are in the next chapter.)

Common History, Complex Relationships

From common Anabaptist roots to a twenty-first-century patchwork of Indiana groups, the Amish stories of migration and movement have been integral to their history and self-understanding. Not only the memory of European persecution that gave rise to the Amish church and propelled its members across the Atlantic but also the specific stories of migration to Indiana have shaped the contemporary color of Amish life.

Indeed, memory is portable, and the patterns that emerge from the history of Amish migration reveal lines of affiliation and connection that follow migration trails more often than simple geographic proximity. Amish families in one part of Indiana may know more about the Amish in a settlement 600 miles away than they do about those living fifty miles down the road. For a people deeply formed by history and memory, the ties that bind are neither easily unwound nor quickly redirected.

But migration history is not the only way to understand the Indiana patchwork. Equally important is the role of church order and discipline in the lives of people who believe that faith should inform all aspects of life. That conviction provides another common thread to the Amish story, but its varied application also adds to the diversity of plain living.

THREE

MAINTAINING THE OLD ORDER

From a distance, the patchwork of the Old Order world can sometimes look more like a puzzle. Why, for example, do the Amish reject telephones in their homes but not in their shops and businesses? How do Old Orders decide what new devices or opportunities they will adopt or adapt? And just how does change happen among a people who carefully regulate innovation?

The more one observes and learns, the more complex the pattern becomes. Mainstream North Americans who prize individual choice find it intriguing that Old Order people would willingly surrender some of their autonomy to the dictates of tradition and the wisdom of the group. But why does the church concern itself with the details of daily life at all? And why do some practices vary from community to community? Why, for example, do Amish women in Adams County, Indiana, wear black head coverings, while coverings almost everywhere else are white? Why do the Amish in some settlements have bicycles, while other church districts—perhaps even neighboring ones—prohibit bike riding?

A closer look at Indiana's Old Order communities only makes their diversity more apparent. The variety in dress, occupations, and everyday practice is striking. Yet behind this mixture of customs are important cultural threads that help explain Amish life and choices even as they bring order to the quality of Amish diversity.

Threads That Bind the Fabric of Old Order Life

One key to understanding the logic of Amish group life is the concept of Ordnung. A German word, *Ordnung* is closely related to the word *order* and refers to the way things are done, the way one goes about everyday life. But Ordnung has implications beyond this literal meaning. It represents the Amish conviction that there is a divine order in the world, that God wants people to live in community and harmony, and that submitting to this corporate order promises more contentment than an individualistic search for meaning on one's own. This ordered picture of life comes from the Amish reading of the Bible, interpreted through the lens of practical folk wisdom and proven tradition.

Ordnung, then, is a way of life—or, more precisely, a way of going about life. It includes both general principles such as modesty and simplicity, and very specific applications such as acceptable styles of hats and bonnets, taboos on higher education and military participation, or refusal to own televisions and radios. The Ordnung is not a published rulebook or written code of conduct but rather an oral tradition, often communicated by example.[1] In this sense the Ordnung is informal yet still widely understood and binding.

Understandings of Ordnung were so important to Amish identity that in the mid-nineteenth century Amish leaders

An Amish "bench wagon" or "church wagon" in Allen County is parked outside a home that will host church the next Sunday. The wagon contains the benches and *Ausbund* hymnals used in worship, and the plates and flatware used for the noon meal that follows. Each church district lives by an agreed-upon discipline known as the Ordnung.
PHOTO BY THOMAS J. MEYERS.

from across the United States convened a series of ministers' meetings to discuss its meaning in an American society undergoing rapid and profound change. How would the Amish respond to a culture that celebrated the autonomy of the individual, or to the growing American tendency to think about church life in terms of organization, programs, and institutions rather than in terms of the daily conduct of the local congregation? In all but one of the years from 1862 and 1878, Amish ministers and bishops met to discuss such matters. Two of the gatherings were held in Indiana.[2] Though the meetings aimed at finding a common understanding of church Ordnung, in the end they only confirmed the disunity that existed among nineteenth-century Amish churches.

Many Amish, it turned out, were warming up to popular promises of human progress, or embracing religious revivalism that placed more emphasis on the individual than on the church. Some leaders suggested staving off the inroads of the outside world by formally codifying and printing the Ordnung, but such a scheme troubled traditionalists, who saw such plans as undercutting the local and informal nature of church order which they held to be as important as its content.

By the late 1860s the tradition-minded Amish leaders had quit attending the gatherings, content to concentrate on serving their local communities while their change-minded compatriots focused energy on adapting to modern life. The change-minded majority, who represented about two-thirds of the North American Amish at the time, looked for renewal through new programs—denominational conferences, publishing houses, formal mission work, schools for higher education, and the like. In the twentieth century these groups, each in their own way, merged with similarly progressive Mennonite bodies and gave up their public Amish identity.

In contrast, the remaining, more tradition-minded Amish ended the nineteenth century committed to maintain the old Ordnung—the old order—and became known as the *Old Order Amish*. But even though keeping the old order set them apart from their change-minded cousins, the Old Order Amish were not free of diversity. Indeed, their commitment to a locally regulated, orally perpetuated sense of Ordnung meant that the old order would necessarily include variety from one context to another.

Ordnung in Action: Boundaries and Change

The Old Orders believe that Christianity is not simply a spiritual experience but also has practical and social dimensions. Faith commitments affect everything from how one dresses to the way one goes about daily work. Religion is not private, individually oriented, or a Sunday-only affair. It is public and community-centered, and it affects all of life.

Ordnung checks the desire to focus attention on the self—whether through wearing jewelry and fashionable clothes or through the shrill claims of individual assurance of divine salvation. Living within the Ordnung encourages modesty and a quiet humility before a God who alone knows the future.

Technology that promotes the autonomy of the individual and freedom of choice, such as in-home telephones or personal automobiles, is also taboo. Yet in all but the most ultra-conservative settlements, the Ordnung permits the practical use of community phone booths or the hiring of non-Amish van drivers for certain trips. In such cases, individual autonomy is tempered and the Amish person must be prepared to work in cooperation with others.

Although the Ordnung is never static or frozen, in the Amish world the burden of proof is always on change. When Amish church districts formally reaffirm their commitment to a corporate, disciplined life twice a year, innovation may be discussed but change is not accepted unless it is supported by a broad group consensus. While bishops and ministers bear a special responsibility for upholding the Ordnung and guiding discussion of change, they typically are not the sole decision makers when it comes to introducing or resisting innovation. Instead, changes emerge only after much conversation—both

Ordnung informs all aspects of Amish life, including the particular shape
and style of one's buggy. This buggy reflects the Nappanee Ordnung and
publicly demonstrates its owner's compliance with church standards.
PHOTO BY JOEL FATH.

formal and informal—has taken place within the community
and the entire church membership has reached agreement on
the new direction.

Another factor influencing the direction and pace of change
is the opinions and wishes of surrounding or related Amish districts. Some church districts may intentionally forego change—
despite their inclinations to the contrary—in order to remain in
fellowship with more conservative-minded churches.

Some aspects of life are more resistant to innovation than
others. For example, farming has long been central to Amish
life and has a cherished history in Amish communities. As a

result, the Ordnung surrounding agricultural practices is more resistant to change, even in settlements where many Amish men work in highly mechanized jobs or hold other off-farm employment. To outsiders this incongruity may seem puzzling. Yet from the Amish perspective, the logic is clear: it is precisely the traditional component of farming practices such as the use of horse-drawn equipment that makes them so significant, and modifying them undercuts the value in farming as a way of life. Accepting changes and adaptations in nonfarm jobs, by contrast, is not nearly so threatening to Amish identity since these other occupations are not closely associated with what it means to be Amish. Simply put, being a printer or a forklift driver is so marginal to the history and meaning of being Amish that such jobs can absorb much more innovation and flexibility than can farming. Thus an Amish shop owner may market state-of-the-art products and take orders on a business phone, while his neighbor plows with horses and shocks corn by hand—and both are living within the bounds of the Ordnung.

Similarly, since the Amish strive to preserve and protect family life, Ordnung involving activities in and around the home is often more resistant to change than the Ordnung surrounding other aspects of life. Some things permitted at a job location away from home may not be acceptable in or around the home itself. Telephones are a good example of this distinction. Some Amish communities permit phone use so long as the device is kept out of the home—in a shop, barn, or phone booth some distance from the house. A few churches may even permit cell phones for checking a business answering service or placing orders from a remote job site, but not for making direct calls from one home to another.

Moreover, the details of the Amish Ordnung may differ

The interior of this Elkhart County home illustrates the local district's Ordnung, including prohibitions on wall-to-wall carpeting and window curtains. The pressurized gas lamp provides light in lieu of electric fixtures. A limited number of decorative items appear on the walls, but not photographs of people. PHOTO BY DOTTIE KAUFFMANN.

from church district to church district within a single settlement. Local tradition, the central role of the church district, and different contexts all shape the evolution of change. Most church districts in northern Indiana's Elkhart-LaGrange settlement, for example, permit bicycle riding, but some do not. Each of the more than one hundred districts there has reached its own decision on this and many other specific issues.

In most cases daughter settlements maintain the same Ordnung as their parent settlement. For instance, the Parke and Wayne County settlements, composed of Amish immigrants from Pennsylvania, have continued the use of gray buggies in the size and style used by their Lancaster kin. Other aspects of the Ordnung in Parke and Wayne also parallel the Lancaster pattern, though there are a few exceptions, such as the Parke County Amish prohibition of tobacco, which is tolerated back in Lancaster.

Old Order Variety

One way to make sense of Indiana's Amish patchwork is to consider its various affiliations—those networks of church districts that share a similar (or even identical) Ordnung and recognize one another's discipline. Significantly, districts within a given affiliation can exchange ministers for Sunday worship and participate in one another's communion services. Districts within an affiliation say that they are "in fellowship" with the other districts in the affiliation. Unlike settlements, which are defined by geography and history, affiliations can span communities and include districts in various locations. Likewise, it is possible for several distinct and non-fellowshipping affiliations to coexist within the same settlement.

The patchwork of Indiana Old Orders includes a number of different affiliations. The *oldest settlements*—Elkhart-LaGrange, Nappanee, and Kokomo—along with the newer Rochester and Vallonia settlements, and the Milroy community, are all in fellowship with one another and form the largest affiliation within the state, representing more than 60 percent of Hoosier Amish. This affiliation is not limited by state boundaries, of course, and these settlements are also in fellowship with the majority of Amish in other parts of the United States and Canada.

What is distinctive about these Indiana settlements though— in contrast to Amish settlements in Ohio and Pennsylvania—is the degree of diversity in Ordnung that exists within this affiliation. Examples abound. Some church districts in these settlements have used bottled gas for cooking and heating since the 1920s, while others have only recently permitted this energy source. Most districts permit subscriptions to secular newspapers, but a few do not. Automatic milking machines—once a taboo in most districts—are now accepted by the majority of churches. But that innovation occurred over time and on a district-by-district basis, not as the result of a settlement- or affiliation-wide decision. Amish farmers in Kokomo use tractors in their fields, while all other churches in the affiliation do not. Architecture, occupations, and levels of interaction with the public also vary significantly within this affiliation. Indeed, a willingness to accept a modest range of differences across the settlement has become a characteristic feature of this affiliation.

The Amish settlements in *Allen* and *Adams Counties* and their related daughter settlements form another circle—or, more accurately, several circles—of affiliation. Fellowship among these Amish traditionally has hinged much more on the notion of all districts maintaining an identical Ordnung. Churches in these affiliations fellowship only with those districts that observe the same Ordnung and that do not introduce change unilaterally; to do otherwise is to provoke a schism. For example, in the Hamilton settlement in northeastern Indiana's Steuben County, married men must be employed at home in a small business or in farming. If one of the districts in that settlement were to permit working away from home, it would cause a break in fellowship within the settlement's affiliation.

At times such situations have developed. In 2002 in Adams County, for example, there were Amish districts representing five different affiliations within the same settlement. Each of the five has a somewhat different Ordnung, and as a result none are in fellowship with the others. The small Vevay settlement in the southeastern corner of the state also contains two different affiliations.

Several smaller affiliations are present in Indiana, too. Southern Indiana's Orange County is home to a community of *Swartzentruber* Amish, an affiliation concentrated in Ohio and including daughter settlements in eleven other states. Since 1913 the Swartzentrubers—nicknamed for two early leaders—have been among the most traditional of all Old Order affiliations.[3] Clothing styles are notably conservative, including items such as especially large bonnets for women and very wide-brimmed hats for men. Homes do not have indoor plumbing, farmers milk cows by hand, and telephone use is sharply curtailed since the church prohibits the community phone booths popular among most other groups. Swartzentruber buggies are simple, without windows or storm-fronts.

In addition to their especially traditional approach to personal adornment and technological innovation, the Swartzentrubers have maintained a number of old cultural customs long associated with American rural life. These include the use of tobacco and traditional courting rituals among young people. Like the unmechanized farming practices that mark Swartzentruber agriculture, these customs are an accepted part of life that, from the Swartzentruber perspective, have always existed.

The Swartzentruber Amish suggest a link between holding the line on technological change and resistance to tampering with traditional folkways. But not all associations are so straightforward. Adjacent to Indiana's Swartzentruber settlement is the *Paoli* Old Order Amish community—one that represents yet another affiliation. Since 1957 this settlement has combined a rigidly conservative stance on technological innovation with a desire to reform other equally traditional customs.

Originally from northern Indiana and Pennsylvania, the Paoli Amish were dismayed with the social and economic changes taking place in their home communities, including increasing attention to material comforts and the rise in factory employment. As a result, the Ordnung of the Paoli settlement includes very plain dress and notably limited use of technology. Windmills are still a common means of pumping water, for example, rather than the gasoline engine pumps found in many other parts of the state. Married men must farm or work at home in small family-centered shops. Families rarely travel to town. Like the Swartzentruber buggies, those of the Paoli Amish do not have storm-fronts or battery-operated lights. Also like the Swartzentrubers, the Paoli Old Orders hire non-Amish van or car drivers only in the most pressing of circumstances.

Yet in ways quite unlike their tradition-minded Swartzentruber neighbors, the Paoli group has staunchly opposed older customs surrounding traditional courtship practices or adult smoking habits. The Paoli settlement is notable for this combination of intentional traditionalism and intentional reformism. Their refusal to compromise on issues they deem important has led them to not affiliate with any other Amish settlements in the state.

Still another affiliation with concerns for closely monitored teen activities and attention to "clean" living is the *New Order Amish*, a network of church districts scattered across thirteen states and tracing their beginnings to 1966 in Ohio. Unlike the Paoli Old Orders, though, the New Order Amish have a

Ordnung guidelines govern the use of the telephone, though the particulars vary from settlement to settlement and in some cases from church district to district. In the Amish church southwest of Salem telephone use is relatively permissive, as illustrated by this advertised phone number.

PHOTO BY THOMAS J. MEYERS.

greater openness to change and are considered the most progressive affiliations in Indiana.[4] Indiana's two New Order communities near Salem and Worthington are small and have primary ties to larger New Order settlements in Bellefontaine, Ohio, and Holmes County, Ohio.

In one sense the New Order Amish are simply another affiliation of Old Order Amish.[5] The New Orders all make use of horse-drawn transportation on the road, dress plainly, and reject many marks of technological modernity such as public utility electricity. But in other ways the New Order Amish are a distinctly different affiliation within the Amish world. For example, New Order groups are more self-conscious about theology, publishing booklets outlining their beliefs and sometimes speaking of "assurance of salvation"—a sort of individual faith claim that more traditional Old Orders see as a misguided human attempt to speak for God. New Order Amish also express interest in gaining converts from non-Amish backgrounds. While they do not have formal missionary organizations, they take special interest in corresponding with religious seekers and make an effort to accommodate outsiders. For instance, while their biweekly church services typically are conducted in the Pennsylvania Dutch dialect, New Order folks will switch to English if non-Amish visitors are present. They also offer midweek meetings for youth and Sunday school classes on the Sundays between their biweekly church services. In terms of technology, New Orders have been more open to innovations such as in-home telephones and have somewhat less traditional standards of dress.

Beyond the Bounds of the Old Order

Given all the diversity of Amish lifestyle and practice among the various Old Order affiliations and their differing approaches to Ordnung, what are the limits of Old Order identity? How much innovation—how much adaptation to modernity—is possible within Old Order circles? Are there Amish who are not self-consciously Old Order?

One such group is the so-called Beachy Amish (nicknamed for early leader Moses Beachy).[6] The Beachy Amish Church began in 1927 in Pennsylvania, but the first Indiana Beachy congregation formed in 1940 near Nappanee, eventually taking the name Maple Lawn Amish Mennonite Church. Today there are fourteen Beachy Amish congregations in the state, mostly located in communities that are also home to Old Order settlements. Although the term Beachy Amish is widely used to identify the group, none of the congregations use that designation on church signs. Congregations are more apt to have names such as Berea Fellowship or Woodlawn Amish Mennonite.

The initial issues that sparked the formation of the Beachy Amish included a desire to do away with the social component of church discipline known as shunning and to allow greater flexibility toward the adaptation of technology. Especially since the 1950s, the Beachy Amish also have become known for their active evangelization and mission work in North America and overseas.[7]

Beachy Amish congregations meet weekly for worship in simple church buildings. Church services are in English, as is most other daily communication in Beachy circles. They stress modesty in dress but are less distinctively plain than Old Orders. Beachy women wear head coverings, and men have closely trimmed beards. Objecting to the content of mass media broadcasts, the Beachy Amish households do not have televisions or radios, but they own automobiles, have in-home telephones, and make full use of public utilities. While some Beachy Amish young people complete high school, most do not. Many Beachy Amish men work in industry or operate small businesses; a few farm. The church discourages women from working outside the home.

On a number of counts the Beachy Amish are not Old Order. Their approach to faith is more rational—that is, more consciously articulated and stated in fairly personal terms. They are more at home with the language of individual salvation than with Ordnung. Formal Sunday school programming, Bible schools, and a more articulate approach to belief also set the Beachy Amish apart from the less introspective Old Orders for whom faith is not enhanced by verbal description or defense. And the Beachy Amish are much more open to the world of technological innovation.

Still, many Beachy Amish see themselves as heirs of an Amish heritage, and some have close family ties to neighboring Old Orders. Some Beachy and Old Order Amish cooperate in joint endeavors. In northern Indiana and in Daviess County, for example, some Old Order people financially support Christian Aid Ministries, a Beachy Amish–related world relief organization. Other Old Orders help with the Haiti Relief Auctions that are organized by Beachy Amish and conservative Mennonites to fund church work in the Caribbean. Nevertheless, all sides agree that the Beachy Amish are not Old Orders.

An Ordered Life

To the outsider the Amish variation in practice and lifestyle—from who uses what kind of telephone to why power lawn mowers are accepted in one church district but forbidden in the neighboring one—may still seem complex, but understanding the role of Ordnung and recognizing various affiliations within the Old Order world helps clarify the patterns amid the similarities and differences that are so striking.

Deference to tradition and the claims of memory shape Ordnung in binding, yet often in very local ways. For the Amish this makes sense and is itself an expression of the larger way of life that Ordnung represents. Making sense of the rich reality of Indiana Amish life requires sensitivity to the dynamic of Ordnung and the seriousness with which the Amish regard its ability to link faith and life.

While many Amish are concerned not simply to merge faith and custom, they believe that Ordnung gives practical shape to the disciplined Christian life. Within that mix of faithful living, of course, ethnic culture and custom do play central roles. Those patterns, explored in the next chapter, add another layer to the Old Order patchwork.

FOUR

AMISH ETHNICITY
Pennsylvania Dutch and Swiss

To be Amish is to be a member of the Amish church. Although onlookers sometimes mistakenly think that the Amish are merely a quaint ethnic group perpetuating a collection of traditional customs for the benefit of tourists (a sort of "living history" pageant), or that someone could become Amish simply by buying a buggy and a set of plain clothes, the Amish understand their identity to be that of a church whose religious beliefs animate their lives. Inquiries about whether one can be a "nonpracticing Amish" or whether one could be Amish without being a member of the Amish church make no sense to them.

At the same time it is clear that the Amish way of life, its strong system of family ties, and its concept of separation from the world are all distinct enough to create a sort of identity that many observers would call *ethnic*. Ethnicity commonly means a shared sense of group identity based on culture, language, or national origin. In the North American context, the Amish often appear to be another of society's many ethnic groups.

Yet the Indiana Amish patchwork actually includes two distinct ethnic groups—two broadly defined traditions of custom, language, culture, and shared history. Two ethnic streams flowing within a common religious heritage highlight the Amish distinction between church membership and culture. Settlements representing these two ethnic groups are another way one can sort the Amish diversity within Indiana.

The "Pennsylvania Dutch" Amish and the "Swiss" Amish

In some ways the two ethnic traditions parallel the two main immigration streams that brought the Amish from Europe to North America. Those Amish who arrived in Pennsylvania in the 1700s were part of a larger German subculture that became known as Pennsylvania German, or more commonly, Pennsylvania Dutch. As described in chapter 2, descendants of these Amish immigrants made their way to Indiana in the years after 1840. More recent Amish arrivals to the state—such as those who started new settlements in the 1980s and 1990s— have also come from communities with Pennsylvania Dutch roots, whether in Ohio, Pennsylvania, New York, or elsewhere.[1] The Swiss Amish ethnic stream, by contrast, was fed by those immigrants who left Switzerland and the Swiss borderland areas during the 1830s to 1850 and settled in Allen and Adams Counties, Indiana.

While the *Pennsylvania Dutch* and *Swiss* ethnic tags mark real and distinct traditions, the labels themselves are less important than what they represent. In many ways the Swiss Amish are no more tied to Switzerland than the Pennsylvania Dutch Amish; nor did all the ancestors of today's Pennsylvania

This farm in Adams County is home to a Swiss Amish household whose ancestry stems from nineteenth-century immigrants to Indiana.
PHOTO BY THOMAS J. MEYERS.

Dutch spend much time in Pennsylvania. Nevertheless, these labels have come to mark the two cultures, even as both ethnic streams have also absorbed people of different backgrounds.

As ethnic groups, the Swiss and Pennsylvania Dutch traditions include not only different histories of migration but also distinct language dialects, customs, and other practices. Certain surnames predominate in each stream and are much less common or altogether absent in the other. Table 4.1 illustrates the different family names found in each group.

Formal and informal interaction between Swiss and Pennsylvania Dutch Amish is less common than interactions among settlements of the same ethnic group. Marriages between Swiss and Pennsylvania Dutch partners—while possible—are rela-

Table 4.1. Typical Indiana Amish Family Names

Pennsylvania Dutch settlements	Swiss settlements
Miller	Schwartz
Yoder	Hilty
Hochstetler/Hostetler	Graber
Bontrager/Borntrager	Lengacher
Lehman	Schmucker
Troyer	Eicher

tively rare. A few families have ties to both groups, but most do not. Business contacts and work on matters of mutual concern such as Amish parochial schools might link people from both groups, but for the most part the twin ethnic streams run in distinct courses. A notable exception is the Milroy community. In recent years a significant number of Swiss Amish have moved into this once predominately Pennsylvania Dutch settlement. Now Swiss names are becoming more common in Milroy, as is the Swiss dialect and the presence of visitors from the Swiss Adams County settlement.

While there are Swiss Amish settlements in a number of states—including Missouri, Michigan, Ohio, Pennsylvania, and New York—the majority of Swiss Amish live in Indiana.

Language and Dialects

One of the major distinctions between the two Amish ethnic streams is language—each group speaks a different German dialect. Those of Pennsylvania Dutch extraction speak a dialect they call *Pennsylvania Deitsch*. The Swiss Amish label their dialect *Swiss*, though it is not identical to the language spoken in Switzerland today.

Pennsylvania Dutch is an American-derived dialect that emerged in the 1700s as Germans from a variety of territories along the Rhine Valley mixed their Old World dialects in their new Pennsylvania environment. Originally the Amish were only a small part of those who used this evolving dialect—the bulk of Pennsylvania Dutch speakers were Lutherans or Reformed. By the twentieth century, however, these groups had largely abandoned the dialect, whereas the Amish and some conservative Mennonites retained it and have come to represent almost all of today's remaining Pennsylvania Dutch speakers.[2]

The dialect spoken by the Swiss Amish is one carried from their Swiss and Swiss-borderland homes to North America. While all languages change over time, Swiss Amish speech did not grow out of an American mixing of dialects in the way that Pennsylvania Dutch did. Still, Swiss speech does vary slightly from settlement to settlement, and the Amish themselves note that the Swiss spoken in Adams County is distinct from that spoken in neighboring Allen County.[3]

These two dialects—Pennsylvania Dutch and Swiss—are different enough that most Amish have some difficulty understanding the other dialect. For example, if a Swiss person from Berne, in Adams County, meets a Pennsylvania Dutch speaker from Shipshewana, in LaGrange County, they likely will resort to conversing in English. Amish with contacts in both ethnic groups report that, given enough interaction, Swiss people tend to pick up Pennsylvania Dutch, but Pennsylvania Dutch speakers rarely learn Swiss.[4]

The German dialect is the first language of all Amish children and is the spoken language of the home. Although most Amish people can read standard "high German," they have widely varying abilities to speak or write high German. Church services are a mixture of high German and dialect. Texts from the Luther translation of the Bible and the *Ausbund*, the Amish hymnal, are read and sung in high German, but ministers preach sermons in the dialect.

To be sure, the Amish are bilingual and are fully fluent in English, but English and the dialect serve different roles in Amish life. Even though Amish parochial schools are conducted in English, it symbolically remains the language of the outside world. Indeed, the Amish typically refer to non-Amish individuals as "English people."[5] At the same time, since Pennsylvania Dutch and Swiss are spoken dialects and do not have standard written forms, the Amish use English for writing letters (even to one another) and doing other clerical work.[6] Amish-published magazines like *Family Life*, and the community correspondence newspapers *The Budget* or *Die Botschaft*[7] are both printed in English. Some church leaders use German to write about spiritual matters, since for them the vocabulary associated with such topics comes from the familiar German Bible.[8]

Open Buggies, Yodeling, and Wooden Grave Markers

While the spoken Pennsylvania Dutch and Swiss dialects are important ethnic markers, these two traditions differ in other folkways and customs as well. Among the most obvious to the casual observer is the style of horse-drawn vehicles. Swiss Amish drive open buggies that do not have enclosed tops; riders in Swiss buggies sit in the open air. The Pennsylvania Dutch–speaking communities, on the other hand, generally drive buggies that have some sort of covered enclosure, even though they might occasionally also drive open wagons or

This Swiss-style unenclosed buggy in the Steuben County settlement near Hamilton is typical of buggies in other Swiss communities. The schoolhouse in the background was an abandoned public school that the Amish have purchased for their own use. PHOTO BY THOMAS J. MEYERS.

carts for some specific purposes. There are many smaller ways in which buggy styles vary from settlement to settlement, but the open or closed carriage distinction is an easily recognizable ethnic difference.

With some notable exceptions, the Swiss generally have been more conservative in their approach to dress, technological change, and innovation. They have tended to stick with traditional power sources such as windmills or small engines rather than adopt hydraulic power or energy from compressed air that has been accepted in many Pennsylvania Dutch districts. These limits have affected the sorts of occupations Swiss Amish men pursue.[9]

Some Allen County Swiss-style buggies, like the one here, include a feature known as a "kid box"—a small, enclosed compartment behind the seat that provides protected seating for small children during inclement weather. Otherwise, riders in Swiss buggies simply carry umbrellas during rainy or snowy conditions. Kid boxes are also used in the South Whitley community, but not in other Swiss settlements in Indiana.

PHOTO BY THOMAS J. MEYERS.

A distinctive characteristic of the Adams County Swiss Amish has been their practice of marking graves in their cemeteries with plain wooden stakes bearing merely the initials of the deceased.

PHOTO BY THOMAS J. MEYERS.

Some Swiss Amish have also maintained a European tradition of yodeling. The practice is most common in Adams County, where the repertoire of yodels includes folksongs such as "Mi Vater ist en Appenzeller" (My Father is from Appenzell), or lyrics wistful for the Alps. The Amish in North America have composed a few original yodels, but many are of Old World origin. The words are playful or reminiscent and not particularly religious in nature. Yodeling is a form of recreation for some Swiss Amish families, but it is unknown in the Pennsylvania Dutch–speaking settlements.[10]

Still another notable tradition among the Swiss has been the custom of marking graves with narrow wooden stakes that include only the initials of the deceased. While all Amish settlements reject large decorative gravestones, the Pennsylvania Dutch communities typically have erected modest stone markers that include full name, death date, and lifespan of the deceased. The traditional Swiss Amish practice, by contrast, symbolizes the fleeting nature of human life on earth. The inevitable deterioration of the wooden stakes denies any permanent memorialization.

Two Cultures

Although to an outsider the similarities between the Swiss and Pennsylvania Dutch–speaking Amish may be more obvious than the differences, the two ethnic streams represent, in some sense, two different cultures—two sets of values about the church and the world. Describing culture is a tricky business since so much of its significance lies in its unspoken assumptions about life and faith. Generalizations are liable both to highlight distinctions and to overlook key exceptions. Nevertheless, Amish and non-Amish observers note certain persistent tendencies in these two Amish ethnic streams.

For example, the Swiss have tended to understand the vitality of the life of the church in terms of uniformity. They often have resisted diversity in practice and lifestyle within a settlement even when such resistance results in a schism and the formation of competing affiliations within a settlement. In addition, the Swiss typically have vested more authority in their bishops as decision makers and agents of church discipline. While these characteristics certainly do not adequately summarize the Swiss approach to church life, they are somewhat in contrast with the habits of most of Indiana's Pennsylva-

This new home was constructed in 2002 by a family in the small but growing Swiss Amish settlement east of Salem. Many families here have roots in Adams County and are part of a network of ethnically Swiss settlements in the state. PHOTO BY STEVEN M. NOLT.

nia Dutch–speaking Amish. The culture in that ethnic stream has tended to understand unity in terms of fellowship among church districts. Their approach has often meant that they are willing to accept more diversity in practice within a settlement in order to avoid division. The practice and implication of excommunication also tend to be different in the two groups.[11]

While members of the two Amish ethnic traditions hardly see themselves as rivals in terms of religious faithfulness, they sometimes stereotype the problems of the other group. Many of these stereotypes, such as each group's view of the other's application of church discipline, are rooted in the limited interaction between the groups and the way rumors sometimes circulate. At the same time, there have been some important cooperation and close friendships linking Amish people across ethnic lines. Pennsylvania Dutch and Swiss Amish leaders, for example, worked together to win legal recognition of Amish parochial schools and to negotiate conscientious objector status with the U.S. military. Ministers in one group may ask their counterparts in the other for counsel. In recent years bishops from the Pennsylvania Dutch–speaking Nappanee settlement have been invited to assist in mediating conflicts in some Swiss communities.

Nevertheless, the two Amish ethnic streams have remained fairly distinct in Indiana and show few signs of blurring into one another. Even the positive interaction that does occur often ends up highlighting ethnic distinctiveness. For example, as a young adult, Swiss Amish John L. Schwartz (1890–1993) of Adams County moved to Nappanee, where he served the church as a minister and bishop for nearly 77 years. Despite decades in this Pennsylvania Dutch–speaking northern Indiana community, the well-loved and respected Schwartz never lost his Swiss accent and was widely known throughout the settlement for his distinctive-sounding sermons.

Beyond Ethnicity

Although to some extent Amish culture follows ethnic lines, the church cannot be reduced to its ethnic heritage. The Amish, after all, have maintained their Anabaptist convictions regarding adult baptism: no one is born into Amish church membership. Just as teens and young adults in the Amish community choose to join the church through baptism, people of non-Amish backgrounds have also been incorporated into Amish churches. The formal process of joining the Amish church—participating in catechism and baptism—is the same for those who grew up with the tradition as for those who did not. Yet Amish assumptions about the many connections between faith and life or about church membership and submission to community are challenging notions for many moderns to accept. Then too, as a practical matter, to fully participate in the Amish community one eventually needs to learn Pennsylvania Dutch or Swiss and become comfortable with other cultural elements of ethnicity.

Nevertheless, throughout the years the Amish have attracted a few converts—some drawn from a distance and others who were neighbors or employees on Amish farms and who saw church members' lives up close. During the 1700s and 1800s, when Amish life and values diverged less sharply from that of other rural North Americans or when large numbers of German-speaking immigrants shared common folkways with the Amish, the decision to join the Amish church may have seemed somewhat easier.

Lambright, now a common Amish surname in northern Indiana, was not always so. Jacob Lambright (1840–1881?)—progenitor of the Amish Lambrights—was a six-year-old Lutheran immigrant to Canton, Ohio, with his widowed father and seven siblings. Eventually needing to support themselves, Jacob and a brother moved to LaGrange County, Indiana, where they found jobs with local families. Jacob worked on an Amish farm, and in 1863 he joined the Amish church. Later he married an Amish woman, Sarah Yoder (1844–1919). New names have also entered the Swiss communities. Girod, now a common Amish name in Adams County and several of its related settlements, first entered Amish circles in 1905 when Samuel Girod (1881–1966), a local Reformed Church member was baptized into the Amish church. Other common Amish family names—including Burkholder, Chupp, Knepp,

Schmidt, Whetstone, and Wickey—all descend from nineteenth-century converts.

Individuals of non-Amish background continue to consider joining the Amish church. In some ways, given the growing gap between Amish values and the modern celebration of individual rights and self-determination, the choice today is more stark. The Amish generally encourage those who express interest in joining their church to live among them for a time and "see what our life is like."

It is always possible for outsiders to join the Amish, but because of the commitment and conviction required, it is never simple. Those who have joined in recent years have almost all been young single men or in a few cases young married couples. Some were local residents who had grown up with Amish neighbors; others bring metropolitan backgrounds and university degrees. Some first became acquainted with the Amish through mutual interests in horses or farming.

In either case—whether converts from "the world" or children raised in Amish homes—the practical expression of Christian faith takes shape in the ordinary habits of life that shape ethnicity. Faith does not float freely in a cultural vacuum. It is embodied in the customs that have emerged and evolved over time, transported across migrating miles and perpetuated via the oral understandings of Ordnung.

Swiss and Pennsylvania Dutch patterns of life reflect these understandings in different ways and, along with settlement history and church Ordnung, mark the contours of Amish interaction with their neighbors, schools, government, and regional economies. Underneath all of these interactions, however, is a basic set of household relationships. For the Amish in Indiana and elsewhere, family and community are the daily arenas of faithfulness.

FIVE

COMMUNITY AND FAMILY LIFE

On Sunday mornings throughout Indiana, Amish families rise early to prepare to attend church. If it is their turn to host the district's worship service, they have been busy all week cleaning, preparing food, and arranging the church benches in a portion of their house, barn, or shop building in anticipation of the two hundred or more people they can expect. Families begin arriving at the host's home as much as an hour before the official nine o'clock starting time, intent on greeting other members and meeting visitors from other church districts or settlements. As buggies pull into the lane and family members descend from their carriages, each person joins his or her age and gender group. Mothers join women who are finalizing preparations for the simple noon meal that will follow the service. Fathers join the circle of men in the barnyard, approaching each brother with a hearty handshake and a kiss of fellowship. Young men and women form their own groups and will enter the church service at the last possible moment, maximizing their social time together.

In a church service the family unit merges with the church community and is not reconstituted until the family is ready to return home well into the afternoon. During the service itself and the meal that follows, men sit with men and women with women. Teens spend the whole morning with their respective gender groups. Here church and family—the most important institutions in Amish life—come together in rituals that bolster community, draw on tradition, and rehearse discipline. Although the details of design vary, the warp and woof of church and family are mainstays of the fabric that forms Indiana's Amish patchwork.

Amish Worship

Older men and women begin moving toward their assigned benches in the ordinary space that has become a sacred site because the church is gathering there.[1] Middle-aged mothers and fathers—some with small children in tow—take their places next, followed by teens. As soon as the congregation begins the first hymn, the ministry—bishop, ministers, and deacon—who have been seated to face the assembling congregation, get up and file out of the room. They will meet briefly in a nearby room where the bishop leads a prayer and offers spiritual admonition, and they will decide who among them will preach that morning. They may also discuss any business that needs to be addressed in a members' meeting after the service. If, for example, a matter of discipline is under consideration, the bishop will request that at the conclusion of worship all non-members be dismissed and the "brothers and sisters" remain for a meeting.

Amish worship follows a prescribed pattern that has been

repeated for centuries. The service opens with two hymns from the sixteenth-century *Ausbund*. The second hymn is always the "Loblied" (Praise Song), number 131 on page 770 of the *Ausbund*. For the Amish, singing this well-known song is a moving experience that links them with other Amish through time and across the country.[2]

Sometime during the singing of the "Loblied," the ordained leaders return from their meeting and one of the ministers rises to give an introductory sermon lasting about a half-hour. At the conclusion of this sermon another minister reads the assigned chapters of New Testament scripture, recites a prayer, and then preaches a second sermon that lasts an hour or more.[3] The preacher concludes by asking the other leaders who are present to comment on or correct anything he has said, and they each take a turn in offering such testimonies. The service ends with a hymn, a prayer, and a benediction.

If Amish worship services are lengthy and formal, they also are simple and plain. There are no religious symbols or images present in the house, barn, or shop where the service takes place, although a clock may be placed strategically in a rafter or on a back wall so that the minister can see it. The Amish never use musical instruments to accompany their hymns, which are led by an experienced male song leader who simply leads the congregation from his seated place among the other laymen. After worship the space is again transformed as some benches become tables and others are arranged around them to serve the simple noon meal provided by the hosting family. Not everyone can eat at once, and people eat in shifts with their respective age and gender groups.

Weekly patterns of worship are interrupted only by specially modified services such as those preceding the semiannual communion services and the communion Sundays themselves, when the service lasts most of the day as ministers recount the story of God's saving acts from creation to the death and resurrection of Christ.

Gatherings to ordain new leaders are also serious and somber events. If a minister or deacon dies or if advanced age keeps him from completely fulfilling his obligations, district members may nominate candidates to fill the role. The final selection is left up to God, however, as candidates draw lots to see who is chosen. At the conclusion of a special worship service, a specially prepared set of hymnals—one for each candidate—is arranged on a table before the congregation. One of the hymnals contains a slip of paper. The candidates each choose a book, and the one who chooses the hymnal with the paper takes it as a sign of divine calling to lead the congregation. Bishops are selected in the same way from among the ministers.

When Family and Community Intersect

If the church is the center and source of Amish identity, the family still serves as the basic building block of Amish society. At the heart of any Amish community is a dense network of interrelated families. Members gather for church in a house or other building on the homestead, not a meetinghouse that is removed from the center of family life. The Amish typically talk about the size of a church district in terms of its number of families rather than the number of individuals. And since only baptized members may marry in the church, the decision to join the church as a young adult is often tied to the choice of a marriage partner, again linking family and church concerns.

In Indiana the average number of families per district varies

Table 5.1. Average Number of Households per Church District

Settlement	
Adams	25
Allen	47
Daviess	47
Elkhart-LaGrange	31
Kokomo	25
Nappanee	27
Mean for six oldest settlements	40

Source: Recent settlement directories.

from settlement to settlement, somewhat based on the usual size of the community's homes. Allen and Daviess Counties have the largest districts, averaging forty-seven households per church. The Swiss Amish community in Adams County, in contrast, averages only twenty-four households per district, in part because of the nature of district division there. Normally new districts form as a result of membership growth, but the Adams County average is pulled down by the fact that some districts there have split because of internal conflict, not because of numeric increase. Controversy can have other results as well. In the mid-twentieth century the Amish settlement near Kokomo experienced discord that led to loss or out-migration of many members. As a result, that settlement—though one of the oldest in the state—still has only two church districts today.

In many places Amish church districts are becoming more compact as fewer families farm and more live on smaller tracts

A recent phenomenon in the densely populated Elkhart-LaGrange settlement is a sort of Amish suburbia, with subdivisions of Amish tract houses. Lots are often too small to include a traditional household produce garden, though each property has a small horse barn and pasture yard. These homes often reflect the lifestyle and income of husbands who work in area factories. PHOTO BY THOMAS J. MEYERS.

of land closer to one another. The rise in Amish population and new housing patterns have increased the Amish population density and shrunk the geographic size of many districts. In fact, in the area around Shipshewana in the large Elkhart-LaGrange settlement, a phenomenon of "Amish suburbs" has emerged—neighborhoods laid out in grids like any suburban development, but with homes that are occupied almost exclusively by Amish people. These lots are typically a bit larger than those in non-Amish subdivisions so that there is space for a horse barn and small pasture, and there are no amenities such as sidewalks or streetlights. But the most striking feature of

In the late 1990s Amish families from the northern part of the state began a new settlement near the southern Indiana town of Vallonia, and several constructed log homes. Few of the households are farming, but they wanted a more rural and sparsely populated setting. PHOTO BY THOMAS J. MEYERS.

these communities is their nearly complete separation from the agrarian way of life, with household heads working in local industry or local shops.

The Amish in Allen County are closer to a major city than is any other sizable Amish community in North America.[4] Here families live within five miles of Fort Wayne's nearly two hundred thousand inhabitants and have access to a wide array of large stores and businesses, although major highways and traffic congestion can make access by horse and buggy difficult.

In contrast, many of the newest settlements in southern Indiana exist in sparsely settled areas. For example, the newest community, established in 1996 near the small town of Vallonia, has only about a dozen families.[5] Families in newer settlements also tend to live much further apart from one another than is common in the older, more densely populated communities. In the small settlement near the southeastern town of Vevay, families are spread out over the hilly terrain of Switzerland and Jefferson Counties. As new families arrived in communities like Vevay, they purchased properties that were available even if they were not in close proximity to the other Amish residents.

Family and Married Life

If population density and church district size vary from settlement to settlement, some characteristics of Amish life are rather constant. While the age at which men and women in the general U.S. population marry has risen steadily into the mid-twenties, Amish young people have continued to marry in their early twenties. Indeed, the five oldest settlements in Indiana show remarkably consistent patterns (see table 5.2).

Amish marriages are not arranged, and young adults may choose whom they wish to marry, but both partners must be church members to be married in the church. Marriage is not limited to members of one's own church district but is almost always to someone from a church that is part of the same affiliation.

An Amish wedding is typically held on a weekday and follows a format much like a standard Sunday worship service.[6] The order of worship is the same, but the focus of the sermons is on marital relationships, drawing particularly on examples of husbands and wives in Scripture, such as Abraham and Sarah. At the conclusion of the service, the couple exchanges vows in a

Table 5.2. Age at Marriage by Gender

Settlement	Men	Women
Adams	22	21
Allen	22	21
Daviess	21	21
Elkhart-LaGrange	22	21
Kokomo	23	22
Nappanee	23	22

Source: Recent settlement directories.

prescribed manner and then spends the day visiting with family and friends over large meals at noon and in the evening. This is perhaps the one day in an Amish person's life when he or she is the center of attention. A great deal of time and energy goes into planning the details of meals, seating arrangements, table ornamentation, and gifts for attendants.

Husband and wife assume traditional and defined gender roles. The man is the religious leader in the home as well as the primary source of the family's livelihood. The wife is understood to be primarily the homemaker. Amish couples assume that there will be many children in their homes, and they eagerly anticipate each childbirth, welcoming the newborn with a great deal of joy. Early in life children begin to work alongside their parents in the home, on the farm, or in the family business.

Although most Amish families are large by general American standards, family size varies a bit from settlement to settlement. The smallest number of children in a family is in the Kokomo community, where women bear an average of six chil-

Table 5.3. Average Number of Children for Women over Age 45

Settlement	
Adams	9
Allen	8
Daviess	8
Elkhart-LaGrange	7
Kokomo	6
Nappanee	7

Source: Recent settlement directories.

dren in the course of a lifetime; and the largest family size is in Adams County, where the average number of children is just over nine.[7]

Amish families remain sizable in large part because of the Amish reluctance to use contraception. Most Amish believe that children are a gift from God and family size therefore should be left to divine will rather than human determination.

Stages of Childhood

More than their counterparts in wider American society, Amish children pass through a series of distinct and recognized stages of life, each marked by a significant rite of passage. Little children usually remain at home until they are ready for school, usually at the age of six or seven. It is extremely rare for an Amish child to be placed in daycare, and with few exceptions, children do not attend nursery school or kindergarten. When a child starts school, the Amish begin to refer to him or her as a "scholar." Scholars remain in school through age fifteen. At that point they begin to work on the farm, at home, in the family business, or elsewhere for hire. Typically, Amish teen-agers turn their paychecks over to their parents to contribute to the household economy.

At age sixteen Amish teens join the "young people" and begin to move somewhat out from under their parents' control and experience a less restricted life (even though, with only rare exceptions, they continue to live at home with their parents during this time). Many young men acquire their first buggy and become more independent. Since their activity away from home is less supervised, some—though certainly not all—young people view this period as a time of exploration in the non-Amish world. Some may wear fashionable clothes, consume alcohol, or smoke. A few young men acquire driver's licenses and purchase cars.

This aspect of Amish teenage life has attracted notable media attention and popular curiosity among Americans who find it incompatible with their notions of what Amish life should be like and who often interpret it as a sign that Amish society is unraveling.[8] Yet it is significant that this period of exploration—even among those whose behavior differs mark-edly from their parents—takes place in an Amish context, since it always occurs in the company of other Amish teens, never as lone individuals or in mixed groups of Amish and non-Amish young people. Thus, even those Amish teens who wish to get a "taste of the world" do so, paradoxically, in a particularly Amish way—a fact that much of the popular fascination with Amish youth overlooks.[9]

In larger settlements with hundreds of young people, teens may join a specific youth group for the purpose of socialization. Each group has its own reputation, and they vary in their be-havior. In many smaller settlements or in certain church dis-tricts within larger settlements, parents tightly control rowdy behavior. Some Amish see the possibility of tighter parental control as an advantage of living in a smaller settlement with fewer teens and more oversight of young people.

By the late teens, however, most young people, even in more rambunctious circles, return to the rules and regulations of the Amish church in which they were raised. For many, the years of dabbling with non-Amish life makes their decision to join the church more informed. They have experienced a bit of what they are rejecting and know what they are giving up when they make a commitment to the church.

Even if their experimenting as teenagers exposes them to the world, most Amish young people do, in fact, decide to join the church. Indeed, in recent years the percentage of young people who leave the church entirely and opt for an adult life in the non-Amish world has steadily declined. In the Elkhart-LaGrange settlement, for example, less than 10 percent of the people under the age of thirty-five have decided against church membership, whereas the rate was more than 20 percent several generations earlier.[10]

Young adults typically are baptized and become members of the church in their late teens or early twenties. At age twenty-one the Amish describe the young man or woman as having "come of age." They are no longer required to turn their wages over to parents, and they are regarded much more as independent adults, even if they are not married and are still living at home.

Aging and Death

Amish parents assume that they will spend their elderly years living with or near one of their adult children. Amish adults do not "retire" into inactivity, but often by their mid-fifties, parents pass day-to-day responsibilities for a farm or home business to the next generation. Typically they will then move into a *Daadihaus,* or grandparents' house, located near or adjacent to the home of one of their married children. The older man or woman remains a productive assistant at home, on the farm, or by launching a new small business venture.

When a person dies, an area funeral home prepares the body for burial but then returns it to the family home, where a wake occurs for several days. Friends and family gather at the home to view the body and quietly visit with one another.

An Amish funeral is much like a Sunday morning church service, except that little or no singing occurs. The body is buried in a local Amish cemetery. In most communities small stone markers indicate gravesites, although as has been mentioned, some Swiss communities have traditionally used only wooden stakes to mark burial sites.[11]

Amish Women

Unlike women in the dominant North American culture, Amish women have not embraced the women's liberation movement. Indeed, when asked, most express little interest in changing their traditional roles as wives and mothers. Although Amish women do not hold offices in the church or any other organization, few perceive themselves as being repressed. They point out that they have the right to speak in church business meetings and may nominate men in the process of selecting church leaders. Observers note that Amish women generally are very influential in the informal dynamics of decision making in the home or in family businesses.

Because home life functions under a fairly restrictive Ordnung, housewives enjoy relatively few laborsaving devices to help them with their tasks even though their husbands often employ technological innovations at work on a construction site or at the factory. Some Amish women comment on this double standard—greater technological flexibility for businessmen and fewer for housewives—but most defend the difference as important for a healthy environment in which to raise children. Amish women and men see the home as the sacred center of family life, where parents impart understandings of Ordnung to the next generation.

Yet even as women's roles remain traditional, they are not static. In recent decades the most significant changes in Amish women's lives are related to the shift away from agriculture that has occurred in all of the larger settlements. As many men have moved into factory labor or carpentry, some married women also have become entrepreneurs and are producing or selling products such as quilts, baked goods, and fabrics. Other women work alongside their husbands in family businesses that cater to the Amish community or make products for non-Amish consumers. The disposable income that accompanies many of these new economic pursuits has in turn changed other aspects of women's traditional roles. Store-bought prepared and convenience foods are now a staple in many Amish homes, lessening somewhat the amount of time and energy women put into food preparation and preservation.[12]

Occupational shifts have changed the structure of responsibilities within traditional roles as well. In the past, when agricultural labor required the participation of the entire family, the husband was generally at home on the farm every day. Children, particularly boys, were actively involved with their father

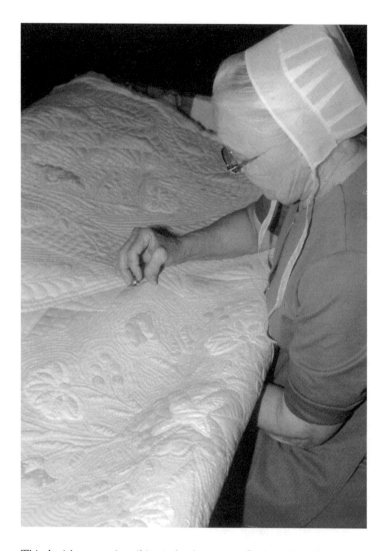

This Amish woman is quilting in her home near Goshen. A traditional skill among Amish women, quilting has recently come to provide not simply attractive bedding for the immediate family but also a product that fetches a good price on commercial markets. Some Amish women have begun their own wholesale and retail quilt businesses. PHOTO BY DOTTIE KAUFFMANN.

This woman rides her bicycle on errands in the town of Topeka, pulling an insulated grocery cart. Such carts have become common in this settlement, where Amish shopping trips frequently include the purchase of prepared and frozen convenience foods. Shifting patterns of production and consumption reflect changing tasks and expectations of Amish housewives. PHOTO BY JOEL FATH.

as a source of labor. More recently, however, in settlements where married men have shifted to work in industry or construction crews that work some distance from home, women have needed to assume responsibility for large numbers of children who have fewer chores. The Amish themselves are ambivalent about these changes. Almost all are quick to cite the potentially negative consequences of absent fathers and choreless children, but they also concede current economic realities and contend that mothers have always been the heart of home life.[13]

Although the assumed role in life for most Amish women is that of wife and mother, some never marry, though few live by themselves. Most single women are absorbed into their extended family, often living with and caring for aging parents. In comparison to the larger society in the United States, where 26 percent of the population lives alone, there are far fewer single-person households among the Amish.[14] In 1995 in the Elkhart-LaGrange settlement, for example, only forty-seven women (2 percent of the 2,697 households) were never married and lived alone in their own home. Even though they live independently, these women interact closely with other relatives. Often they have a small house on the edge of parents' or siblings' property.

Yet recent decades have witnessed an important shift in the vocational lives of single women. Table 5.4 shows occupations of single women in the Nappanee settlement.[15] In the past, single women typically found employment in non-Amish homes doing housework or caring for children and the elderly. However, currently the overwhelming majority (90 percent) of women engaged as domestics are over age sixty-five. Instead, factory work has become a preferred option for younger single women, giving them more economic independence.

Throughout Indiana, church and family remain central elements of Amish life, even if some aspects of these institutions vary from place to place and economic realities are modifying parts of a traditional way of life. Changing or changeless, these institutions reflect and perpetuate Amish values. From hymns that recall the sixteenth century to family systems that focus on

Table 5.4. Occupations of Single Women in the Nappanee Settlement

	N = 58	%
Factory Employment	23	40
Non-Amish Business	11	19
Housekeeping	10	17
Unemployed*	4	7
Quilting	3	5
Home Health Care	2	3
Sewing	2	3
Other	3	6

*These are elderly women; one resides in a nursing home.
Note: Data in this table do not include single women living with their parents or those who are widowed. The data represent only those women who are listed in single-person households.
Source: Owen E. Borkholder, comp., *Nappanee Amish Directory, including the Rochester, Kokomo, and Milroy Communities, 2001* (Nappanee, Ind.: O. E. Borkholder, 2001).

rearing children who will join the church, the Amish world of submission, humility, and traditional authority shines through church and household, and—not surprisingly—binds them together in numerous ways.

Yet the Amish also live in environments that are in many ways hostile to their values, and their struggle to live productively within their local contexts is also an important part of who they are and who they have become in the modern world. Local contexts and the many Amish responses to them are part of the patchwork of their lives, shaping the ways they educate their children, find employment, and interact with neighbors.

SIX

AMISH SCHOOLS

In the fall of 1921, eleven Amish men were arrested in northern Indiana's LaGrange County for failing to comply with the state's Compulsory School Attendance Act. Earlier that year Indiana had enacted legislation requiring all children between the ages of seven and sixteen to be enrolled in a recognized school. Some Amish parents—concerned with the nature and content of high school curriculum—kept their high-school-age children at home. Eight years of basic instruction, coupled with practical work experience at home, was all their children needed, these parents reasoned.

The offending fathers were quickly fined $10 and court costs, but their difficulties did not end with this experience. As late as November 1924 the *LaGrange Sentinel* reported that Amishman Emmanuel Miller was again being fined for violating school attendance laws, and trouble continued for several more years.[1]

These were neither the first nor the last cases of conflict between Amish parents and state officials over matters related to proper schooling, and tensions in other Indiana communities continued for decades.[2] In 1948 in Jay County, Chester Gingerich, a father of thirteen children, was fined $200 and sentenced to sixty days in prison for refusing to send his fourteen-year-old son to high school. Gingerich was later pardoned by the governor, but he was taken into custody again the next year for the same offense. This time Chester's brother Perry was also arrested for refusing to send his sixteen-year-old son to high school.

The Indiana Supreme Court eventually settled the Gingerich brothers' case and—to everyone's surprise—interpreted the attendance requirement as applying only through age fifteen, thereby clearing the Gingerich cousins and their fathers.[3] Yet the saga of conflict between Indiana Amish parents and school officials continued. In the fall of 1950, following the closure of all the rural public schools in Jay County's Green Township in favor of a distant consolidated school, Amish parents took the then-unusual step of opening their own school on Perry Gingerich's farm. Local officials immediately challenged the validity of the school, and in 1954 they arrested Chester Gingerich for sending his nine-year-old daughter to a noncertified school.[4]

Clash of Cultures

What lay behind this series of confrontations? What was the objection of the Amish parents to aspects of public education, and what motivated local officials to press the issue? In the early twentieth century, civic-minded individuals, eager to modernize America, believed that formal education would lead the nation into a bright new future. Even in rural communities the education of farmers was thought to be key to increasing agricultural production.

For local schools, the incentive to maintain high enrollments was often linked directly to government subsidies: the more students enrolled, the more dollars local schools could expect for their budgets. In July 1924 the *LaGrange Sentinel* ran a front-page story about the decline in state funding for public schools as a result of decreasing student enrollment. The story included the rumor that LaGrange schools were in such dire straits that they might close for part of the year.[5]

It is easy to see why non-Amish school administrators were uneasy about the Amish position on public education. But why were Amish parents averse to sending their children to high school? The Amish reluctance to allow their children to go to school beyond the eighth grade grows out of several concerns. Most Amish assume that the practical skills of reading, writing, and arithmetic learned in the first eight grades provide sufficient skills for any child to succeed. Moreover, the critical thinking associated with higher education can easily become an end in itself, encouraging some children to question the faith and values of their parents. Indeed, advanced schooling offers the temptation of worldly ambition and pride.

High school may also expose children to instrumental and performance-oriented music, to classes that emphasize individual expression, or to art classes that require students to draw human faces.[6] The Amish are also uncomfortable with physical education classes that require what they consider immodest apparel and the use of public showers. And they are particularly uneasy about science or health classes that include presentations on human sexuality, a subject they believe should be handled at home rather than at school, especially when it

Students in an Amish school in Elkhart County. Statewide, as many as 5,500 children attend Amish schools. PHOTO BY DOTTIE KAUFFMANN.

is taught by non-Amish teachers who may not share Amish values. Other classes, such as biology, may emphasize the theory of evolution, which is not consistent with the Amish understanding of creation.

Finally, Amish parents are aware of the power of popular teen culture in high schools and do not want their children to have daily association with non-Amish peers. As one Amish father noted, "We are taking dangerous chances if we expect our children to mix with the world and not be harmed by it. . . . For the world, education is training the mind for success in this life. For the Christian, education is training the child to live for others, to use his talents in service to God and man, to live an upright and obedient life, and to prepare for the life to come."[7]

Added to these concerns was the midcentury trend toward

public school consolidation, especially in rural areas, which solidified Amish suspicions.[8] Amish parents watched their children bussed to distant schools staffed by teachers they did not know and who were unfamiliar with their culture. Since the Amish prefer organizations that are small enough that everyone knows everyone else, they favored small schools where the teacher is known by all of the parents and where the parents know one another and the other children. In large schools, Amish parents feel they have no influence on decisions affecting their children. They may have only infrequent contact with school personnel. Furthermore, consolidated schools are likely to be well beyond walking distance from the child's home, and parents prefer to see their children walk, bike, or drive a pony cart to a school that is no more than a mile or two away from home.

The Emergence of Amish Parochial Schools

Although Amish families had supported their local public schools for years, a growing sense of concerns, coupled with deeply held convictions, led some parents to consider establishing private, Amish-run schools. The shift to Amish schools was neither immediate nor complete—in some settlements Amish children still attend public schools today—but the move toward private education as a means of passing on academics and Amish values had begun.

The first private school in Indiana for the exclusive instruction of Amish children opened its doors in 1948 in northeastern Elkhart County. In the 1950s more schools followed in Nappanee (1951), LaGrange County (1957), and Allen County (1959).[9] At first, Amish parents bought and refur-

In 1948 this abandoned public school just east of Middlebury reopened as Indiana's first Amish parochial school. Renamed Plain View School, it has been extensively remodeled and is still in use. PHOTO BY THOMAS J. MEYERS.

bished abandoned one-room public schools, but eventually they ran out of such options and started constructing new one- or two-room buildings. Initially, parents also believed that they would need to hire non-Amish teachers or perhaps send their own teachers to high school and college for certification, but state officials conceded that was not necessary.[10]

Nevertheless, the state often was uneasy about the Amish school movement, and in certain places it tried to block the establishment of these private schools. After authorities in Allen County repeatedly issued subpoenas to parents of Amish children enrolled in private schools, the Amish there organized to negotiate with state leaders. In 1967, under the leadership of David Schwartz, an Amish school committee formed with representatives from the Allen, Adams, Daviess, Elkhart-LaGrange, and Nappanee settlements. State Superintendent of Public Instruction Richard Wells, who was sympathetic to the needs of parochial schools, met with the group at an Allen County Amish schoolhouse and played an important role in helping the Amish develop a proposal outlining the nature of Amish schools to present in Indianapolis.[11]

Since Amish parents wanted to avoid sending their children to high school, the initial goal of the Amish State School Board was to formulate a so-called vocational school plan modeled on an arrangement Amish parents in Pennsylvania had negotiated with their government. Under that plan, Amish children who had completed eighth grade but were not yet fifteen attended school for several hours of basic skills review each week until the child's fifteenth birthday. During this time the student also kept a journal of his or her work activities at home, which an Amish teacher read. The agreement between State Superintendent Wells and the Amish incorporated aspects of this vocational plan.

After the state granted the Amish the right to establish their own schools, David Schwartz wrote a succinct set of school guidelines. This document outlines the management and supervision of teachers by an Amish school board, proper deportment of teachers and students, and careful maintenance of school records, particularly regarding attendance. The Amish set as their goal an attendance rate of 97 percent and have had no difficulty in maintaining this commitment to the state.

Even though Amish schools exist in every settlement in Indiana, some Amish parents continue to opt to send their children to local public schools—though only through eighth grade, and not to public high schools. This is particularly true in the older communities, where generations of Amish students attended public schools prior to the beginning of the Amish school movement. In these places a fair amount of good will continues to exist between public school teachers, administrators, and the Amish. Some Amish parents believe the public schools are academically superior and will better prepare their children for adult occupations.

Nevertheless, the percentage of Amish children enrolled in public schools has continued to decline. During the late 1970s in the large Elkhart-LaGrange and Nappanee settlements almost half of Amish children attended public schools, yet by 2001 only 40 percent in Elkhart-LaGrange did so. The drop around Nappanee was even sharper, with only about 20 percent enrolled in public schools in the early twenty-first century. In more recently established Amish settlements in central and southern Indiana, where parents had no longstanding ties to the public schools, all Amish children attend private Amish schools.

The Organization of an Amish School

While Amish society is by no means frozen in time, education in Amish schools is much closer to the one-room schoolhouse of late-nineteenth- and early-twentieth-century America than to the assumptions of modern consolidated schools. In the majority of Amish schools all grades meet in one or two rooms. Since typically one or two church districts support each school, Amish schools are truly community schools, and children can easily walk, ride a bicycle, or take a pony cart to a school.

Each school has a governing board, typically made up of

Most Indiana Amish schools have two classrooms with multiple grades in each room. Teachers encourage collaborative learning.
PHOTO BY DOTTIE KAUFFMANN.

three fathers of children in the school. In a conscious attempt to keep the sacred role of the ministry separate from the secular role of school administrator, ministers do not serve on the school board. The board hires the teacher, pays the teacher, and makes sure that regular parent-teacher meetings are held.[12] The board is also responsible for the care and maintenance of the school building.

Amish parents are expected to take an active role in the school. In addition to paying a tuition fee, they are expected to visit school regularly to observe the class and to attend school meetings. If parents choose to send their children to public schools, they are not obligated to support the local

Amish school, but some of these families make contributions, nonetheless.

Typically, teachers are Amish young women, or occasionally young men, who themselves have only an eighth-grade education. They are hired because of their skills in working with children but also because they have a good moral character and are able to command the respect of their pupils and the pupils' parents. Among the most important attributes of an Amish teacher is the ability to run an orderly and disciplined classroom.[13]

Amish Expectations

One of the primary functions of an Amish school is to teach children proper English. Parents know that the German dialect is fine for the Amish community, but as adults their children will need to interact with an English-speaking public. No matter what occupation they choose, learning to speak English is so important that many schools impose a penalty for speaking German dialect on the school grounds.

Although parents want their children to learn basic skills in addition to English, they also expect that their children will be schooled in an educational environment that is consistent with their home, and while the teacher's job is not to teach religion, parents assume that teachers will respect and uphold Amish values. Teachers should teach these core values implicitly and by example, rather than by an explicit exegesis of Scripture. As one school manual suggests,

> Teaching the Golden Rule and to sacrifice and get along with each other is just as important as any lessons from books. Respect for authority, respect for the school and

other property should be taught, as well as respect for each other. Those who offend should be taught and required to make things right. If the teacher makes a mistake, even if not purposely, a sincere apology goes a long ways to gain and keep the respect of the school.[14]

Parents expect that Amish values will be incorporated in all school activities. For example, although there is no formal physical education class, there is always plenty of exercise at recess. Amish children play games with great gusto, but there is little emphasis on competition, winning, or singling out star athletes.

Finally, parents believe schools should be places of order. They expect that the school building will be kept neat and tidy. The children assist in daily cleaning and in such tasks as carrying wood for the stove or taking out the stove ashes. An Amish teacher should have the same sense of propriety as an Amish homemaker. Children should be quietly at work, and the physical space should be orderly.

Effectiveness of Amish Schools

In an effort to measure the effectiveness of Amish schools, anthropologists John A. Hostetler and Gertrude E. Huntington gave Amish children standardized tests and compared the results with a control group of public school students. They discovered very little difference in the performance of the two groups except in the area of English vocabulary and found no evidence to support claims that Amish school instruction was inferior.[15] In fact, in some instances, especially in spelling and arithmetic skills, Amish children's test results were superior to non-Amish public school pupils. The poorer Amish perfor-

Baseball is a common recess game, and both boys and girls participate. Teachers typically make students choose new teams each day so that ongoing competitive rivalries do not form. PHOTO BY JOEL FATH.

mance in vocabulary, the professors suggested, was not simply because English was the Amish students' second language, but also because the standardized tests were timed. Students in Amish schools have little experience with timed tests because their schools discourage time-consciousness and the impulse to hurry by allowing children as much time as they need to complete exams. Amish students worked slowly and carefully but did not always complete these standardized exams in the time allowed.

From the perspective of Amish parents, however, the effectiveness of their schools involves more than simply academic achievement. Schools are to teach Amish values and support parents and the church in raising children in that tradition. On this score too, Amish schools seem to be effective, for research shows that children attending Amish schools are more likely to join the Amish church as adults than children who attend public schools. In recent decades the portion of children who choose to join the church as adults has risen to about 90 percent, and the influence of Amish schools has been part of that increase.[16]

Variations in Indiana Amish Schools

Amish school size varies from place to place, as does the relationship between Amish schools and the public school systems. Among the smallest schoolhouses are one-room structures on very simple lots in the Orange County settlements. While most schools in the state have playground equipment such as swings, seesaws, ball diamonds, and basketball courts, none of these amenities are provided in the very conservative

Table 6.1. Number of Amish Schools, Teachers, and Students, 2002–2003

Settlement	Number of Schools	Number of Teachers	Number of Students	Mean Number of Pupils per Teacher
Elkhart-LaGrange	57	115	2,035	18
Adams	28	53	1,088	21
Allen	6	20	634	32
Daviess	11	22	587	27
Nappanee	19	37	549	15
Parke	6	9	180	20
Wayne	4	4	110	28
South Whitley	1	2	51	26
Rochester	1	2	35	18
Salem/New Order	1	2	34	17
Kokomo	1	3	31	10
Worthington	1	2	27	14

Source: Blackboard Bulletin, December 2002, 13–15. Data for schools in other Indiana settlements were incomplete and are not included here. Special education teachers and classes are not included in the table because they are very small, typically three or fewer students, and would therefore skew the average.

Orange County communities. On the other hand, the largest Amish school in Indiana is in Allen County. With five teachers and about 150 students enrolled in the fall of 2002, it is perhaps the only multistoried Amish school anywhere.[17] There are six Amish schools in Allen County with a total enrollment of 634.[18] These large schools emerged as a result of an agreement with the local public school district to bus the children to the Amish schools. A similar arrangement exists in the Adams

Amish schools in Allen County are unusually large. This five-room building enrolls about 150 students. PHOTO BY THOMAS J. MEYERS.

County settlement, though the Amish there have not replaced their small buildings with larger ones.

Apart from these unusually small and large schools, most Indiana Amish schools are one- or two-room buildings with fifteen to twenty-eight students per teacher. Although many of the Indiana schools are physically larger than Amish schools in other parts of the United States (particularly those in Lancaster, Pennsylvania), the number of students per teacher remains relatively small. Many Indiana Amish schools have two rooms—though in some schools there is simply a partition or piece of cloth hanging from the ceiling to create two rooms. Each room serves four grades, and there are two teachers, one for each room. In the two largest settlements—Elkhart-

This schoolhouse in the especially conservative Amish settlement just east of Paoli is strikingly modest even by Amish standards. There is no large playground equipment or paved basketball courts as are sometimes found at Amish schools in more progressive settlements. PHOTO BY STEVEN M. NOLT.

LaGrange and Nappanee—there are fewer than eighteen students per teacher or classroom. Here the distinct preference for small schools is related to the lack of transportation from the public school system.

In recent years some Amish communities also have begun to accommodate children with special needs. Typically a portion of a regular Amish school building—perhaps a basement or one room in a two-room schoolhouse—is set aside for special education classes for children with learning difficulties. These classes began in the 1980s in LaGrange County and in 1991 in the Nappanee settlement. During the 2003–2004 school year there were twelve such schools in the Elkhart-LaGrange settlement, six in the Nappanee area, and several in other settlements. In Elkhart-LaGrange and Nappanee the Amish have also begun to offer specialized teaching for mentally and physically challenged children, including those with Down's syndrome.[19]

Passing On the Faith

Seen from a legal perspective, the success of Amish schools might be interpreted as an important achievement for religious freedom and civil rights. Still another perspective would highlight the connection between culturally appropriate education and the success of minority students to learn in settings where they are comfortable with their values and expectations.

For the Amish parents who have invested time and money into the establishment of these schools and entrust their children to them, the private schools have been an example of innovation in the service of tradition. Amish schools are a relatively recent phenomenon, but they point to the sort of flexibility and creativity that the Amish exhibit when they are forced to change in order to preserve something they hold dear—in this case, the environment in which their children are schooled.

The economic marketplace has posed problems as potent as those stemming from state education offices. The Amish struggle to manage occupational change has stretched the fabric of Amish life in new and challenging ways.

SEVEN

AMISH WORK
Farm, Factory, Carpentry, and Cottage Industry

I f one thing is common amid the diversity that marks Indiana's Amish patchwork today, it is the shift away from farming as the economic base of Amish communities. In both large and small settlements, old communities and just-established settlements, in remote rural areas and suburbanizing regions—the Amish are moving toward occupations other than tilling the soil. Farmers for generations, the Amish are still associated in the popular mind with agriculture. But today only a minority of Amish households make their living by farming.

Yet if the trend toward nonfarm work is a common theme almost everywhere, the alternatives to agriculture vary from settlement to settlement, and sometimes within settlements. Three clusters of occupations—industrial employment, carpentry and construction crews, and home-based small businesses—attract Amish household heads, but the mix of jobs is different from place to place.[1] For example, although many settlements include no factory workers, in a few places that is the most common type of job for Amish men. These similar trends and different expressions add to the color of Indiana's Old Order patchwork.

A Heritage of Farming

The Amish have long been a people of the land. In Europe they had been among the leading farmers of their day, and they arrived in North America with finely tuned agricultural skills. As religious outsiders, the Amish (and Mennonite) descendants of the Anabaptists were barred from owning land in Europe, and in many places they ended up renting isolated acres well removed from village life. Living on the periphery of society and tilling marginal property drove them to improve weak soils. Already in the early 1700s, less than two decades after the Amish division, followers of Jakob Ammann living near the village of Sainte-Marie-aux-Mines in eastern France, where Ammann had spearheaded the movement, had gained a reputation for agricultural ability. The local prince informed the French King Louis XIV that "the Anabaptists apply themselves with extraordinary care to agriculture, an occupation for which they have admirable knowledge. . . . In the valley Sainte-Marie, they have cleared in the plains as well as in the mountains a very large quantity of land and numerous areas that had never been cultivated or inhabited, and would not have been without them."[2]

Ironically, it was their exclusion from village life that allowed Amish farmers the freedom to innovate, to experiment, and to develop new agricultural techniques. For example, because of their limited access to tillable land, they became particularly proficient at animal husbandry and were adept at raising and breeding dairy cattle. The Amish developed new

A farmer near Middlebury works his fields with six draft horses. Today less than a fifth of the men under sixty-five in this Elkhart-LaGrange settlement make their living by farming. In every settlement except Kokomo, Amish farmers use horses to pull equipment; the Amish near Kokomo have used tractors for field work since the 1940s.

PHOTO BY JOEL FATH.

varieties of plants for grazing, such as clover, that also improved soil quality, making the land more productive and creating more feed for stock. They pioneered practices such as collecting animal manure and systematically applying it to fields and pastures. From well-fed cattle they gained not only meat but also improved milk production, turning to cheese making.[3]

The Amish brought this agricultural expertise and flare for experimentation to North America, often remaining at the forefront of agriculture, and became known as able farmers.[4] The agrarian way of life suited them well, and through the nineteenth and mid-twentieth centuries nearly every Amish family lived on a farm. But a series of economic and social changes gradually began to pull some Amish away from the farm. They were not immune from the impact of the Great Depression on rural markets, and in the 1930s a few northern Indiana young men began taking off-farm jobs in local industry. Other household heads launched farm-related small businesses, and produced some of the first manufactured horse-drawn agricultural implements for Amish who were still tilling the soil. By the 1950s, as most non-Amish farmers shifted to tractors and no longer needed older style horse-drawn farm implements, a small number of Amish machine shops emerged to fill this void.

In the second half of the twentieth century the Amish began to face new problems of shrinking land availability and rapidly growing populations. With an average family size of seven to eight children and a growing majority of these children remaining in the faith of their parents and hoping to farm, land became scarce. At the same time, the growth of non-Amish suburbs and rural housing developments in the older settlements took acreage out of production. Not surprisingly, as land became less available it also became more expensive.

During the 1970s the shift away from agriculture began or accelerated in all the large Amish settlements across North America. Although many Amish expressed regret or even opposition to this trend, most believed they had no choice but to explore other occupational options.

To be sure, some did choose to leave older communities and to venture into less-populated areas of the country—including central and southern Indiana—in an effort to continue their farming tradition. Such motivation was largely responsible for the creation of Indiana's Parke and Wayne County Old Order

Amish families from Lancaster, Pennsylvania, who settled in Parke County began this farmers' market as an outlet for home-grown produce and other products. PHOTO BY STEVEN M. NOLT.

Table 7.1. Change in Average Value of Farmland and Buildings in Selected Counties with Amish Populations, 1978–1997

	1978	1997	Change
Indiana	$1579	$2064	31%
Counties			
Adams	1955	2290	17%
Allen	1974	2699	37%
Elkhart	1769	2738	55%
Fulton	1541	1532	-1%
LaGrange	1320	2418	83%
Miami	1665	1926	16%
Orange	907	1288	42%
Parke	1022	1600	57%

Source: U.S. Department of Agriculture *Census of Agriculture, 1997*, AC97-A-51 (available at www.nass.usda.gov/census/census97/volume1/in-14/in2_06.pdf).

settlements, where families from Lancaster County, Pennsylvania, moved to take advantage of land that was cheaper and more readily available than in more crowded and expensive eastern Pennsylvania. Like their European ancestors who had refurbished languishing farms in France and Germany, these migrants have revived dairy farming and improved neglected soil in these Indiana counties.

But with their focus on farming, the Pennsylvanians in Parke and Wayne Counties, along with the most conservative groups in Orange and Steuben Counties, are the exception to the rule in Indiana. Today only a minority of Amish Hoosiers are directly involved in agriculture, thanks to economic and demographic pressures that have prompted sharp increases

Table 7.2. Occupations of Men Ages 35–64 in the Elkhart-LaGrange and Nappanee Settlements

	Elkhart–LaGrange		Nappanee	
	1995 (N = 1146)	2002 (N = 1519)	1993 (N = 297)	2001 (N = 335)
Farm	37%	26%	17%	12%
Factory	40	41	48	41
Shop	12	17	11	30
Carpentry	4	7	10	10
Other	8	10	13	8

Source: Jerry E. Miller, comp., *Indiana Amish Directory: Elkhart LaGrange, and Noble Counties, 2002* (Middlebury, Ind.: J. E. Miller, 2002); Jerry E. Miller, comp., *Indiana Amish Directory: Elkhart, LaGrange, and Noble Counties, 1995* (Middlebury, Ind.: J. E. Miller, 1995); Owen E. Borkholder, comp., *Nappanee Amish Directory, including the Rochester, Kokomo, and Milroy Communities, 2001* (Nappanee, Ind.: O. E. Borkholder, 2001); and Owen E. Borkholder, comp., *Nappanee Amish Directory, including the Kokomo and Milroy Communities, 1993* (Nappanee, Ind.: O. E. Borkholder, 1993).

in land prices along with often weak commodity markets. And even in places like Parke and Wayne Counties not all the Amish are farmers. Table 7.1 illustrates the trajectory of land prices in the late twentieth century. While the value of land and buildings decreased slightly in Fulton County, they increased dramatically in many other areas of the state, often by more than 50 percent.

Table 7.2 demonstrates the steady decline in the percentage of Amish men who work primarily in agriculture. In contrast to the situation in 1995 in the Elkhart-LaGrange settlement when 37 percent of the household heads age thirty-five to sixty-four listed themselves as farmers, the 2002 directory showed

Opened in 1979, the Deutsch Kase Haus cheese plant near Middlebury was initiated by Old Order Amish entrepreneurs who sought a local market for milk that would help keep dairy farming viable. The plant is not owned by the Amish but buys much of the local Amish milk production.
PHOTO BY THOMAS J. MEYERS.

only 26 percent of such men indicated that they were exclusively in farming. In nearby Nappanee, by the turn of the century a mere 12 percent of men in this age group remained in agriculture.

The most dramatic shift away from farming has occurred among young adults (table 7.3). In the Elkhart-LaGrange settlement only 7 percent of fathers under age thirty-five were full-time farmers. The rate in Nappanee for the same group was a mere 3 percent. It is difficult for many young men to

Table 7.3. Occupations of Men under Age 35 in the Elkhart-LaGrange and Nappanee Settlements

	Elkhart–LaGrange		Nappanee	
	1995 (N = 992)	2002 (N = 1214)	1993 (N = 259)	2001 (N = 269)
Farm	12%	7%	5%	3%
Factory	71	68	71	72
Shop	8	13	8	13
Carpentry	4	8	7	7
Other	6	5	9	4

Source: Jerry E. Miller, comp., *Indiana Amish Directory: Elkhart LaGrange, and Noble Counties, 2002* (Middlebury, Ind.: J. E. Miller, 2002); Jerry E. Miller, comp., *Indiana Amish Directory: Elkhart, LaGrange, and Noble Counties, 1995* (Middlebury, Ind.: J. E. Miller, 1995); Owen E. Borkholder, comp., *Nappanee Amish Directory, including the Rochester, Kokomo, and Milroy Communities, 2001* (Nappanee, Ind.: O. E. Borkholder, 2001); and Owen E. Borkholder, comp., *Nappanee Amish Directory, including the Kokomo and Milroy Communities, 1993* (Nappanee, Ind.: O. E. Borkholder, 1993).

secure a farm, and those who do often struggle to make mortgage payments. In both settlements work in factories has become the most common source of employment for this age group.

The Industrial Alternative

Factory work predominates in the large Elkhart-LaGrange and Nappanee settlements, where it is the most common form of employment for Amish men under age sixty-five and is especially so for those under thirty-five. While a handful of Amish men worked in industry as early as the 1920s, not until after World War II did a significant number take up such jobs. To-

An Amish man in the Elkhart-LaGrange settlement bikes to work at a nearby factory. Industrial employment is the most common form of work in this community and the nearby Nappanee settlement.
PHOTO BY JOEL FATH.

day they constitute a large portion of the labor force in the recreational vehicle and manufactured housing industries that thrive in this part of the state.[5] Outside of these north central settlements, however, Amish work in industry is virtually nonexistent.[6]

In those settlements where it dominates, employment in industry has had a significant impact on Amish society. Factory work can be lucrative for Amish assembly-line workers, and the disposable income of a factory worker in northern Indiana is often considerably larger than that of a farmer. In recent years families with new access to cash are going to restaurants and large discount retailers with greater frequency. Many families are able to take extended trips during vacation periods, typically hiring a non-Amish driver to take them to national parks such as Yellowstone or to the Grand Canyon, combining their sightseeing with visits to other Amish settlements on the way.

Migration away from farm employment has also transformed Amish housing and architecture. Today most young families live on small plots of land, each with a modest home and small shed and pasture lot for their driving horse. The sprawling farmhouse with many rooms designed to house multiple generations is now being supplanted by much smaller dwellings with an adjacent shop building or modest pole barn that may also function as the meeting site for church services.

Traditionally, status in the Amish community had been linked to success in farming, keeping children within the faith, and having family members in the ministry. Today, Amish men working in the factory may receive recognition for particular skills, or they may be asked to assume positions of responsibility as supervisors, crew leaders, or foremen. Thus, a new form of status is emerging for Amish workers who gain specialized skills in the non-Amish work world, for example, earning a reputation for adroit use of the computer on the job. Yet those same computer skills could never be applied at home, since the church does not permit members to own personal computers.

Finally, as noted in the previous chapter, the Amish family is experiencing changes in the wake of the shifts to new forms of employment. Traditionally, agriculture had been a labor-intensive activity engaging all the members of a farm family.

Large families meant that there were more workers available to share the workload. In some settlements, as Amish people begin to leave the farm the average family size is declining slightly, even though it remains high in comparison to that of larger society. For example, the average family size of farmers between the ages of forty-five and fifty-five in the Elkhart-LaGrange settlement is around eight children, whereas families of factory workers in the same age group average only six children.[7]

Other Employment Options

Although factory work dominates Amish communities in the north central portion of the state, some members there have turned to home-based shops and other micro-enterprises. An increasing number of middle-aged and older men are establishing such small businesses, particularly in Nappanee, which has recently witnessed a slight drop in the number of factory workers and a rather dramatic increase in small businesses. Some of these men established themselves financially by working in industry when they were younger and then used their savings to start their own businesses.

Small business has been the most common alternative to farming in a number of other Indiana settlements, including Daviess County, Rochester, and the New Order churches in Salem and Worthington. In these places and in the larger settlements, a wide rage of Amish cottage industries produces and sells a remarkable array of products. Although these shops traditionally have catered to the needs of their own community by providing services such as buggy and harness repair, more and more of these businesses are making products for the non-

A growing number of Amish operate small businesses like this
retail store near Milroy. PHOTO BY THOMAS J. MEYERS.

Amish market. Among the most popular items are wood products, particularly furniture. Other businesses include machine
shops, engine repair shops, firms specializing in plastic fencing,
shipping pallet production, accounting and tax preparation,
lawn furniture production, and fabric and handicraft sales.

Small business owners typically see their at-home firms as a
means of allowing work to remain family-centered and intergenerational, much like farming. Children and older adults can
lend a hand as needed, and husbands and wives often share
bookkeeping responsibilities. In 1995, in fact, Amish leaders in

Table 7.4. Occupations of Men Ages 35–64 in the Kokomo and Milroy Settlements

	Kokomo		Milroy	
	1993 (N = 23)	2001 (N = 26)	1993 (N = 24)	2001 (N = 42)
Farm	70%	54%	45%	24%
Factory	0	0	0	0
Shop	4	19	21	21
Carpentry	13	19	17	48
Other	13	8	17	7

Source: Owen E. Borkholder, comp., *Nappanee Amish Directory, including the Rochester, Kokomo, and Milroy Communities, 2001* (Nappanee, Ind.: O. E. Borkholder, 2001); and Owen E. Borkholder, comp., *Nappanee Amish Directory, including the Kokomo and Milroy Communities, 1993* (Nappanee, Ind.: O. E. Borkholder, 1993).

the Elkhart-LaGrange community who hoped to foster such businesses created a revolving fund to provide interest-free loans to young families who want to start their own home-based businesses. Called the Bruderhand fund, the initiative is designed to "relieve young people from the burden of large debts or the need to work away from home. The goal is to help the young fathers have projects at home in a small way that will lead more to a quiet, simple lifestyle rather than working at jobs away from home which tend to circulate a lot of money and leisure and idle time."[8]

In the Kokomo and Milroy settlements, both small business and carpentry work have become the most common alternatives to farming among older and younger men (tables 7.4 and 7.5). In Milroy, especially, carpentry is growing rapidly as

Table 7.5. Occupations of Men under Age 35 in the Kokomo and Milroy Settlements

	Kokomo		Milroy	
	1993 (N = 12)	2001 (N = 9)	1993 (N = 47)	2001 (N = 38)
Farm	58%	22%	23%	11%
Factory	0	0	0	0
Shop	8	22	23	29
Carpentry	25	33	38	58
Other	8	22	15	3

Source: Owen E. Borkholder, comp., *Nappanee Amish Directory, including the Rochester, Kokomo, and Milroy Communities, 2001* (Nappanee, Ind.: O. E. Borkholder, 2001); and Owen E. Borkholder, comp., *Nappanee Amish Directory, including the Kokomo and Milroy Communities, 1993* (Nappanee, Ind.: O. E. Borkholder, 1993).

the preferred occupation. Although the Adams County Amish directory does not provide occupational data, sources there make it clear that construction has become by far the most common alternative to farming. In part this may be because several of the church affiliations in Adams County observe a strict Ordnung that prohibits certain types of power sources, such as hydraulic or pneumatic power, used by more progressive settlements to operate equipment in home-based businesses. Barred from using this technology in the home, these Amish turn to construction work away from home, where the Ordnung is less restrictive.

Employment in the construction industry is a good example of a symbiotic relationship that has emerged between Amish society and the larger culture around them. Hoping to benefit from their reputation for craftsmanship and reliability, construction firms eagerly hire Amish men who have left the farm looking for a new source of income. Employers also benefit from the fact that the Amish church does not allow members to join labor unions, thus keeping their wage demands lower.

Amish-owned construction businesses are a growing phenomenon. This is possible only when certain strategic agreements are made with non-Amish employees. Since the Amish are prohibited from owning trucks or vans to transport workers and carpentry tools to a construction site, a non-Amish employee must provide a vehicle. This individual might also purchase state-of-the-art electrically powered tools for his fellow Amish construction workers to use on the job. Even if the construction business is Amish-owned, the tools themselves are owned and controlled by a non-Amish employee or business partner, so church members are not prohibited from using them.[9]

Having assembled a mobile unit fully prepared for almost any construction task, some Amish crews find work a long way from their home communities. In some cases they may even leave for days at a time to go to large cities such as Louisville or Cincinnati. On location they might stay in motels and purchase their meals in restaurants.

Employment in construction has led to many of the same changes that are related to employment in industry. Some new Amish homes are more elaborately furnished and are constructed of nontraditional materials. In the Allen County, Kokomo, and Milroy settlements, for example, Amish homes sometimes have brick exteriors or ornamental features such as elaborate plastic fencing, gazebos, and grillwork on front porches. The influence of disposable income and the absence of fathers from the home for long periods of time each workday are also factors for families of construction workers.

The End of Amish Society?

Casual observers and even many scholars long assumed that grounding in agriculture was essential to the continuation of Amish society. Farm life helped minimize contact between the Amish and the larger world, the argument ran, so any move away from the farm would threaten the very survival of Amish society.[10]

Certainly occupational shifts have resulted in *change* for the Amish, but there is no evidence that Amish society is about to disappear because of it. In contrast to middle-class Americans, who frequently find their sense of identity in their jobs, defining themselves by what they do or where they work, Amish identity is grounded in membership in a distinct faith community. They do not, for example, think to introduce themselves to a stranger by saying they are a factory worker or a carpenter—or a farmer, for that matter. Instead, work is a means to an end—a way to survive economically, but not the source of their deepest values. Indeed, despite the changes that have accompanied the move away from agriculture, fewer young people are leaving the Amish community today than in the past when most lived on farms, and children of non-farmers are no less inclined to join the church than those reared in farm families.[11]

Yet change has been a constant for Amish living in the midst of the modern world, and some of the most important developments have involved increased interaction with that larger world. New jobs often have meant new or different relationships with non-Amish neighbors, customers, tourists, professionals, and government officials. The next chapter explores these evolving dynamics.

EIGHT

THE AMISH AND
THEIR NEIGHBORS

One of the enduring myths about the Amish is that they are a reclusive community with little or no contact with the outside world. With more and more Amish spending their days alongside non-Amish co-workers on the factory floor or at the construction site, this image is no longer tenable. Yet even before the rise of nonfarm work, the Amish had frequent, if selective, contact with larger society. Indeed, one of the issues at the heart of the 1693 Amish division itself was how Anabaptists should relate to sympathetic outsiders who offered support in times of intense persecution. From the earliest days of Amish history there have been important relationships with outsiders.

In North America, during much of the nineteenth and twentieth centuries Amish children had almost daily contact with their non-Amish neighbors in rural public schools. Today many older Amish people have fond memories of school days with non-Amish peers, and some continue to maintain contact with these old friends. With the growth of Amish parochial

Amish mix freely with non-Amish neighbors at community events such as this public auction in Elkhart County. PHOTO BY DOTTIE KAUFFMANN.

schools, however, contact with school-age children from the dominant culture has become less common.[1]

Still, relations with "the English" (as the Amish term outsiders) continue through neighborly contacts. In some settlements, in fact, Amish families or single adults live in or near towns such as Bremen, Etna Green, Geneva, Milroy, Middlebury, Monroe, Nappanee, Topeka, and Shipshewana. In some cases these town-dwellers, especially if they are older adults, do not own a horse, since they can walk to stores and other businesses. For longer trips they can hire a "taxi" driver—a local English person who provides transportation, for a fee, to Amish people in the driver's own vehicle.

Beyond such contacts, the most common associations with outsiders today are in the workplace, as service providers on the farm, or as customers at an Amish-owned small business. Other points of interaction occur through tourism, health care, and charitable work and in the occasional Amish conflicts with state and local authorities.

Working Relationships

Even Amish farm families who have lived somewhat away from the hustle and bustle of town and city life have always had regular contact with outsiders who haul their milk to the dairy, sell them seed and fertilizer, and provide veterinary medicine. From time to time Amish farmers also use the services of county extension agents and other agricultural specialists. In recent years some households who have remained in agriculture have done so by developing specialty produce crops such as green peppers, pumpkins, or organic vegetables. Some have formed local cooperatives to market their products and often form relationships with large supermarkets in their area.

Through their cottage industries, many Amish have developed an amazing network of contacts in the business world. Their reputation for honest, reliable craftsmanship has spread, largely by word-of-mouth, throughout the country and to other parts of the world. Some businesses market products internationally, even without the benefits of the latest telephone and electronic communication technology, a prominent World Wide Web presence, or the aid of high-priced marketing firms.[2] Horse-drawn carriages made at a LaGrange County

In relatively progressive Amish communities, including the Elkhart-LaGrange settlement, Amish and non-Amish neighbors come into contact in many commercial establishments and public spaces.
PHOTO BY DENNIS L. HUGHES.

Amish shop, for example, have found their way to Mackinac Island at the tip of Michigan's Upper Peninsula and to the French Quarter in New Orleans. The same firm has sold plows to a customer in New Zealand. An Amish-owned machine shop in Allen County provides brass bells, magnets, and collectors' spoons for the gift shop at the NASA headquarters in Houston, Texas.

A few Amish business owners in the Nappanee and Elkhart-LaGrange settlements have become members of local chambers of commerce and occasionally attend chamber-sponsored events to pick up pointers on marketing or advertising. In settlements observing a more conservative Ordnung, Amish small business owners might still have regular retail or wholesale contacts with non-Amish customers and clients, but they would not join in a formal affiliation with "English" business people.

Tourism

Amish-theme tourism first mushroomed in the 1950s in Pennsylvania as vacationing baby-boomer families from East Coast cities flocked to Lancaster's "Pennsylvania Dutch Country," but soon it spread to Midwestern communities. The first Indiana site was Amishville, which opened in 1968 near the town of Berne and offered the visiting public a tour of a formerly Amish-owned farm. Amish Acres opened near Nappanee two years later and soon grew into a sizable establishment.

In some Indiana communities, tourism has become an arena of significant interaction—even if indirect—between the Amish and the outside world. Five counties have notable Amish-related tourist activity—Adams, Allen, Daviess, Elkhart, and LaGrange—and attract visitors from all over the world. But even smaller settlements like those near Milroy and Paoli attract visitors and have spawned a few tourist-related businesses. Virtually all Amish-theme tourist attractions are developed and maintained by non-Amish businesspeople. In many cases these entrepreneurs have Amish ancestry and are several generations away from their Old Order roots. Amishville, Gasthof Amish Village near Montgomery, Das Dutchman Essenhaus near Middlebury, the Shipshewana Auction and Flea Market, and Yoder's Department Store in Shipshewana are all examples of establishments of this kind.

Tour groups often fan out from such establishments or from

Hundreds of thousands of tourists visit Indiana Amish-theme shopping and destination sites each year. The Amish do not own this or other such establishments. PHOTO BY THOMAS J. MEYERS.

other destination sites to visit smaller Amish settlements as well. For example, in the summer buses regularly leave from the state parks near the southern Indiana town of French Lick to sightsee the back roads of Orange County and its Amish farms.

Tourism has also become a significant part of the local economy in counties with large Amish populations. By the end of the twentieth century tourists were contributing nearly $300 million annually to the economy in Elkhart and LaGrange Counties. Tourism also generated some 4,187 jobs in Elkhart County, more than a thousand jobs in LaGrange County, and some $74 million in tax revenue for state and local governments.[3]

What are tourists seeking as they travel the back roads of Amish country? The answer is not as simple as one might first think. Some tourists clearly are curious about a group of people who appear to have sustained a way of life that has been lost by the dominant culture. But there can be little doubt that tourists also come as consumers, eager to purchase crafts, food, and other elements of Amish material culture.

The town of Shipshewana is one of the focal points of tourist activity in Indiana. As host to one of the country's largest flea markets—a sprawling network of more than a thousand vendors and fourteen acres of patron parking—Shipshewana attracts more than 30,000 visitors each week during the summer months. The town also has a bustling business district, supported largely by tourist traffic, and it is home to Menno-Hof, an important visitor center that provides information about the history and contemporary life of area Amish and Mennonites.

Shipshewana is only one of the towns featured in the local tourist industry publication, which is simply titled *Amish Country Northern Indiana*. The eighty-four-page glossy magazine, brimming with ads for "quaint hometowns" and "heirloom furniture," informs potential visitors that when they stay in a local inn or bed and breakfast, they might hear "the rhythmic clop-clop-clop of an Amish buggy."[4] Consumers come to the region expecting quality in the products they buy because of the strong Amish reputation for craftsmanship. According to the non-Amish tourist bureau publication, "Northern Indiana's furniture craftsmen wield their tradition like a finely tuned tool. Because making furniture that lasts—the Amish way—has its foundation in generations of passing down skills from father to son, from grandfather to grandson."[5]

So are visitors attracted to northern Indiana "Amish coun-try" because they find values that are in direct opposition to the individualistic, consumer-oriented dominant culture? Or are they lured to Shipshewana as consumers on a quest for Old Order products? Less than 20 percent of respondents to a re-cent Shipshewana tourist survey identified the Amish as the most compelling reasons for their trip. Instead, they cited retail opportunities at the flea market, followed by shopping at local craft stores.[6]

Although many tourists expressed an interest in Amish cul-ture and regarded it as part of their attraction to the area, it is also clear that most tourists are looking for consumer goods, expecting to find good quality products there because they as-sociate such quality with the presence of Amish in the area. Asked if the label "made by the Amish" increased their interest in purchasing a product, nearly two out of three visitors said yes, and frequently they added that they believe the label sug-gests "quality" or "homemade" products.

For many tourists, a visit to Amish country also suggests a retreat to a quiet, rural location where they can relax. Here they can observe an alternative way of life from a distance as they pass an Amish buggy in their car, stop by the roadside to watch a farmer at work, or eat in a restaurant with Amish employees. They may also enter staged presentations of Amish schools, barns, or homesteads such as Amish Acres, the well-known visitor center and theatre complex at Nappanee.

How do the Amish respond to tourists? The number of direct encounters between Amish individuals and tourists is relatively small. Some Amish-owned fabric or food shops at-tract tourists as retail customers, but many Amish-owned busi-nesses are wholesale manufacturers or firms that cater to the

Amish community itself and do not draw a tourist clientele. Most Amish who live some distance from major tourist attractions have only occasional and indirect contact with visitors on the road. For the most part, they tolerate the presence of tourists and sometimes express mild dissatisfaction with the number of cars and buses that clog narrow country roads. Occasionally an Amish person will express unhappiness with the way their identity is tied to products that are sold by non-Amish vendors. When a small community in central Indiana that had no Amish residents began to sponsor an "Amish" fair, one Amish man from a different community joked, "If they are going to use the Amish name, we should get twenty-five to thirty percent of the profits!"

Indeed, some Amish strongly resist the commercialization of the Amish name. Soon after Amish from Lancaster, Pennsylvania, began settling in Parke County, Indiana, in the early 1990s, one Amish woman made arrangements with a local grocery store to sell pies. When the business owner put up a sign advertising Amish baked goods, the woman protested and said she would not sell her items under such a sign. The store-owner relented, even though sales did in fact decline without the Amish label. Later the Parke County Amish started a small farmers' market along a well-traveled road, but they do not use the word *Amish* in their signage or advertising.

Sociologist Donald Kraybill has suggested that tourism may actually have a positive effect on the Amish. Tourism has made the Amish aware that the larger society is fascinated by their way of life and that they have become more fascinated as time goes on. "To many Amish," writes Kraybill, "the fact that tourists come from around the world to learn of their ways reinforces their collective identity and values. Reluctant to admit pride, they take a quiet satisfaction in knowing that their culture is worthy of such respect. In this way, tourism bolsters Amish self-esteem."[7]

At a deeper level, Kraybill also suggests that Amish traditions may be reinforced, rather than shattered, by contact with tourism.

> Knowing that tourists come to see a people driving horses and living without electricity reinforces expectation for such behavior. Thus, Amish behavior, in part, fulfills the expectations created by tourism. Such external expectations likely fortify rather than weaken actual Amish practice. To discard the buggy, for instance, would not only break Amish tradition, but it would also shatter the expectations of the outside world.[8]

And to the degree that tourism generates tax dollars for local communities, civic officials may be less prone to antagonize Amish populations in ways that would encourage them to move away.

Health Care

A different sort of interaction results from Amish contact with health professionals. The Amish regularly use the services of modern medical facilities for situations they cannot treat themselves. Like many people in traditional societies, the Amish are not quick to run to the doctor for every ache or pain, and some have a bias toward what they see as more natural remedies represented by herbal supplements. But when a serious injury or an incapacitating illness occurs, few Amish hesitate to seek professional medical attention. Since no Amish person completes high school and enters university, there are no Amish physicians or nurses; thus they must patronize non-Amish doctors and hospitals. Some also draw on the services of non-Amish chiropractors, herbalists, and other practitioners of alternative medicine such as reflexologists and iridologists. A growing number of Amish communities have also become convinced of the need to treat mental illness as a medical disease and are increasingly open to professional help in such cases. Not surprisingly, more traditional affiliations are less open to such approaches. A few mental health care institutions in northern and northeastern Indiana have established Amish-friendly centers for their services, allowing greater involvement of patients' families and working in a cooperative way with the Amish church.[9]

The Amish not only depend on the services of medical professionals, but they also have assisted medical researchers in their work. Because the Amish are a relatively homogenous population and have maintained fairly complete genealogical records, sometimes even traceable to specific European villages, they have been particularly good candidates for genetic research. Researchers have learned much about conditions such as hemophilia, limb-girdle muscular dystrophy, and cartilage-hair hypoplasia through careful studies in which the Amish have been willing, cooperative participants.[10]

The Amish believe that church members should not purchase commercial health insurance but should depend on fellow church members for support instead of corporations that speculate on the misfortunes of others. Thus, the Amish are increasingly vulnerable to very high medical bills that must be paid in cash. In some communities, such as the Elkhart-LaGrange settlement, the Amish have negotiated with local hospitals for reduced rates for cash payments by their people. At both the Elkhart and Goshen hospitals, an Amish patient identifies his or her church district on admission and is entitled to a reduced fee. This system is advantageous to both the Amish and the hospitals. Amish customers must pay their bills in full, in cash, within a month of service. The hospital avoids the administrative costs of billing and receives remuneration for services more quickly than they would through insurance channels.

In the case of especially large medical bills, Amish families may receive assistance not only from their own church district but also from neighboring districts within the settlement or even from churches in other settlements. Deacons play a key role in coordinating and collecting "alms" for such purposes.

Some Amish have also tried to reduce the costs associated with childbirth by developing alternatives to traditional hospital care. In 1996 Amish in northern Indiana established a birthing center known as New Eden Care Center.[11] Opened in August 1997 in LaGrange County with the cooperation of area obstetricians, the center is staffed by certified nurse midwives. Some family doctors deliver babies there as well. Although the Amish do not own the facility, it has a board of directors made up of five Amish men. Overhead costs are minimal, and births cost a fraction of what they do in local hospitals. Women may remain at the center longer after giving birth than they typically are allowed to do in a hospital. Some four hundred children are born at New Eden each year.

Although there are no Amish doctors, a handful of Amish act as herbalists or offer other alternative treatments for illness—both to fellow church members and to many non-Amish clients. Occasionally, local authorities question these practitioners to determine whether they are merely dispensing advice and selling nutritional supplements or have crossed the

LaGrange County's New Eden Care Center is an obstetrics center providing Amish women with an alternative to hospital maternity wards.
PHOTO BY THOMAS J. MEYERS.

line into practicing medicine without a license. In two celebrated cases in the 1980s, Indiana authorities brought charges against a Berne-area Amish iridologist-herbalist and an Amish man near Goshen said to be acting as a physical therapist. In both instances, their clientele included many non-Amish patrons, some of whom had traveled across the country to seek treatment.[12]

Participation in Charitable Organizations

The Amish have always stood ready to help non-Amish neighbors in a time of crisis, whether in the wake of natural catastrophe or from the effects of a prolonged illness. In a more formal way, many Amish people volunteer alongside Mennonites in an organization known as Mennonite Disaster Service that provides relief to victims of natural disasters—no matter what their religious affiliation—and rebuilds homes damaged or destroyed by floods, hurricanes, or tornados. Some Indiana Amish also work with non-Amish volunteers to process and can meat for distribution around the world by the international relief and development agency Mennonite Central Committee (MCC).

In recent years Amish in northern Indiana, in particular, have begun actively to support the work of Christian Aid Ministries (CAM), an Ohio-based agency affiliated with the Beachy Amish and some conservative Mennonite groups. CAM provides clothing, food, and other material aid to meet human need around the world. Members of some church districts regularly volunteer at the CAM warehouse in Shipshewana, sorting and bundling donated clothing, bedding, and shoes. Old Order people are attracted to CAM because it is a loosely organized, non-bureaucratic agency where they personally know the staff and trust that their contributions of money and labor will provide direct relief to needy people. The Amish in Daviess County annually support a benefit auction to raise funds for both CAM and MCC.

Some Amish are also actively involved in a non-Amish–initiated program to aid the impoverished nation of Haiti. Haiti Relief Auctions take place annually in several Amish communities, including Shipshewana; Arthur, Illinois; Mount

Hope, Ohio; Lancaster, Pennsylvania; and Pinecraft, Florida. Old Order auctioneers, accountants, and other assistants are active in this program that raises several hundred thousand dollars each year.

Conflicts with State and Local Government

Although relations between the Amish and their neighbors are usually very good, there have been occasional conflicts with state and local government over such things as property zoning violations or the safety of horse-drawn transportation on public roads.[13] Although the Amish rarely vote and they try to avoid active involvement with government, they do respect the state and believe they must obey all laws that do not violate their consciences. For example, since 1954 Indiana counties have held the option of requiring Amish buggies to be licensed; and in those jurisdictions where licensing is necessary, the Amish comply.[14] (Indiana is the only state to regulate buggy transportation in this way.)

Laws insisting that buggies display a bright orange slow-moving vehicle (SMV) triangle, in contrast, have caused concern among the most traditional Old Orders, who find them ostentatious in color and also believe that their trust and confidence ought to be placed in God rather than in earthly symbols. In the fall of 1968 the Amish in the small and very conservative settlement near the town of Paoli refused to comply with the new SMV requirement. A minister in the community had admonished his congregation "not [to] worry about their own safety. God would take care of them. And if it were His will to let persecution come then He would also give them the needed grace to bear it."[15]

A father and two of his sons from this community went to

Government concern for buggy safety is expressed in the many horse-drawn vehicle signs, such as this one posted along public roads to caution car and truck drivers near Berne. The silhouette on this sign approximates the Swiss-style unenclosed or "open" buggies used in that community. In other parts of the state such signs typically bear a silhouette of an enclosed Amish buggy. PHOTO BY THOMAS J. MEYERS.

jail rather than pay a $100 fine for not having the SMV triangle on their buggies. The following year local authorities—who saw the law as a matter of public safety rather than divine trust—made more arrests, and some Amish served additional jail time. Finally, with the intervention of an outsider (who was of Amish background), the governor agreed to intervene on behalf of the Amish, and the arrests ceased. The Amish community in Orange County and a few other places in Indiana have been granted an exemption from the SMV law; however, the vast majority of Old Orders in Indiana use the SMV symbol and have even been quietly critical of those who refuse it.[16] Conflicts involving zoning ordinances have been more common than those involving SMV emblems. With the rapid growth of the Amish population and their shift away from farming, more and more families have established at-home businesses, often located in rural areas not previously zoned for commercial use. Some settlements in sparsely populated areas of southern Indiana do not have zoning ordinances, but those near urban areas face extensive zoning guidelines. In such places, zoning board meeting reports often include items such as the appearance of "Sam R. Yoder, who asked for a permit to operate a canvas shop at his house . . . [and] was granted permission. The home is in an agricultural (A-1) zone. One of the restrictions is that the business operate between the hours of 7:00 AM and 5:30 PM."[17]

Occasionally such requests for variances are denied, sparking resentment from some Amish entrepreneurs who—correctly or not—feel they are treated unfairly. In a few cases Amish businesspeople simply have begun construction without seeking proper authorization, provoking fines or even the closing of the business. Most Amish business leaders are conscious of the need for civic planning and sympathize with the goals of county code enforcers, but others resist what they feel are arbitrary regulations that work against family-centered work that involves multiple generations at home. Others complain about the costs of compliance and the maze of paperwork.

Some conflicts have prompted conversation with people outside of Indiana who face similar pressures. Members of the

Amish community on the edge of Fort Wayne, for example, have consulted with Lancaster County, Pennsylvania, officials about replicating Pennsylvania zoning ordinances that take Amish needs into account, recognizing "that they are unique [as land users] and regulations need to be written that recognize that uniqueness."[18]

The rise of small business has resulted in some other conflicts with state and federal authorities. Government regulation of air and water quality, workplace safety, and hazardous waste all affect Amish-run businesses. Occasionally non-Amish neighbors who have moved to the country seeking refuge from the noise of city life complain about noise pollution from Amish manufacturing shops in rural areas.

Amish businesses also have periodic encounters with the Occupational Safety and Health Administration (OSHA). Occasionally OSHA has waived certain specific regulations to accommodate Amish religious principles, as for example in a 1972 agreement reached by OSHA and a committee of Amish representatives from settlements across the country that exempts the Amish from wearing hard hats on construction jobs, provided they wear their own church-approved hats.[19] Since OSHA does not regulate businesses that employ only immediate family members, many Amish firms are exempt from OSHA standards because they are small, family-run establishments, not because they are Amish-owned.

A Public Life

Amish interaction with the wider world is hardly new, but in recent years and in important ways it is increasing. Amish-theme tourism continues to grow, and the Amish themselves—especially through their forays into the world of commerce—have encountered government regulation in new ways. Meanwhile, advances in health science have led to the development of new relationships, from partnering in genetic research to seeking creative alternatives to costly care.

If these new channels of connection and conversation have led to greater understanding in many quarters, they have also added to a sense of confusion on the part of some non-Amish observers who are more aware than ever of the diversity of twenty-first-century Old Order Hoosier life. The local orientation and authority of the Amish church means that Ordnung is not uniform across all settlements or even within a single settlement. The willingness or reticence to engage the state, for example, varies notably from one settlement to another. What works as a comfortable compromise in Nappanee may be unacceptable in Paoli. Local contexts, ethnic attachments, and churchly commitments are all important pieces of the pattern for those working with or living near Amish neighbors.

Adding to the richness of this social fabric are the contrasting colors of Indiana's Old Order Mennonites, a smaller group whose comparative presence may in fact be a clarifying complication for those willing to take the time to consider yet another piece of the Old Order patchwork. Looking at both the Amish and the Old Order Mennonites underscores themes common to Old Order life, while it highlights those elements that are particularly Amish.

NINE

A DIFFERENT PART OF THE PATCHWORK
Indiana's Old Order Mennonites

While the Amish are the best known of Indiana's Old Order people, they are not the only horse-and-buggy-driving plain people in the state.[1] A smaller number of Old Order Mennonites also live in two northern Indiana settlements—one near the town of Wakarusa and the other close to Tippecanoe.

To area visitors and even longtime neighbors, the differences between the Old Order Amish and Old Order Mennonites can be confusing. In Elkhart County, for example, both groups drive black buggies, wear decidedly plain clothing, and speak Pennsylvania Dutch. Both support a system of parochial schools that ends formal education with eighth grade. No wonder many observers mistakenly lump the Old Order Mennonites under the Amish label.

Like the Amish, the Old Order Mennonites are faithful representatives of an old order way, committed to a disciplined life of faith in community and skeptical toward the modern promise of progress at any price. Yet they live their convictions in a Mennonite mode that is in some ways quite different from their Amish neighbors. Understanding both groups helps highlight common old order values as well as the more distinctive characteristics of each church.

The Old Order Movement among the Mennonites

The same cultural pressures that produced an old order movement among the Amish also did so among the Mennonites. Rejecting the authority of the past and the constraints of tradition, nineteenth-century American society championed the free individual and placed trust in a competitive marketplace of popular ideas. Americans also began to measure religious success in organizational terms—seeking to build larger and more complex church institutions to manage tasks that once had been the preserve of the family and local congregation. For Anabaptist heirs who saw Christian faithfulness in terms of right relationships and imitation of a humble Christ, the new cultural scene was alien and alienating. When it seemed to begin permeating Mennonite church life, some Mennonites—like their Amish religious cousins—dissented.

One such dissenter was Jacob Wisler (1808–1889), a Pennsylvania-born minister and later bishop who had moved to eastern Ohio and then in 1848 to Indiana's Elkhart County. Three years earlier, Mennonites had begun settling in Elkhart County around an area known as Yellow Creek, roughly halfway between the town of Goshen and what would become the village of Wakarusa. Wisler was one of several leaders in the Yellow Creek Mennonite Church who, during the later 1860s, debated the merits of cultural and religious change. Fellow minister John F. Funk (1835–1930) strongly favored denomi-

Indiana's Old Order Mennonites living near Wakarusa and Tippecanoe use horse-drawn transportation for travel on the road but allow tractors for farm work. PHOTO BY DOTTIE KAUFFMANN.

national innovation and pioneered church publication, Sunday school conferences, and organized mission work. Wisler was not so sure, believing that such enterprises sacrificed more than they gained in the process of church renewal.

By 1872 the regional Mennonite conference expelled Wisler, charging him with holding back the advancement of the church. But almost a quarter of the Yellow Creek members backed Wisler, and they began meeting separately for worship as the first Old Order Mennonite congregation.

Like the Old Order Amish, the Old Order Mennonites questioned the value of specialized programs and bureaucracy in shaping church life. For example, they favored Christian education in the context of family or multigenerational church

This Old Order Mennonite buggy, while different in style from that of any Old Order Amish group, represents a similar commitment to a traditional way of life that stands apart from modern social values.
PHOTO BY THOMAS J. MEYERS.

services rather than in Sunday school programs which were designed and taught by specialists and which segregated children by age and rewarded their performance with prizes. The Old Orders endorsed the traditional Mennonite Ordnung as defined in the conference discipline and were cool to the showy personal and household adornment gaining popularity among other Mennonites. While individual elements of innovation might not be inherently bad, snubbing the wisdom of the community flew in the face of humility that Old Order folks prized. As one Old Order member explained, "There's nothing wrong with the English language, but when [Pennsylvania] Dutch folks want to be English, that's pride."[2]

Old Order Mennonite settlements. MAP BY LINDA EBERLY.

Table 9.1. Old Order Mennonite Settlements in Indiana

Settlement	Origin	Number of meetinghouses
1. Yellow Creek (Elkhart County)	1845	3
2. Tippecanoe (Marshall-Fulton Counties)	1992	1

Nevertheless, the old order that these Yellow Creek Mennonites upheld was a *Mennonite* tradition, not an Amish one. Thus, they continued the traditional Mennonite practice of worshiping in church meetinghouses rather than in private homes like the Amish, and they upheld Mennonite patterns of dress and appearance. Old Order Mennonite men are clean-shaven, for example, in contrast to bearded Amish men. Old Order Mennonites do not practice Amish-style shunning of the excommunicated, though they do take church discipline seriously. In short, the Old Order Mennonites and Old Order Amish came to share a general old order outlook and penchant for plainness while differing in the details of how that locally maintained order should be expressed.

Jacob Wisler's circle of churches soon included not only those in northern Indiana but also tradition-minded Mennonites in eastern Ohio's Wayne County and northern Michigan's Emmet County. Nor was the Indiana-Ohio-Michigan Wisler fellowship alone in its sentiments. Old Order Mennonite churches later emerged in Ontario (1889), Pennsylvania (1893), and Virginia (1901), though the movements in those areas were distinct from Wisler's Midwestern fellowship.

The Old Order Mennonites in the Midwest have experienced a number of painful divisions over how best to put Christian faith into practice. They are not proud of these schisms, but the disputes have shaped the way in which their church maintains its common life. In 1907, for example, Midwestern Old Order Mennonites split over the question of telephone technology. Indiana bishop John W. Martin (1852–1940) led those who rejected the phone as a threat to local community life and interaction. In the years that followed, the Martin group also held automobiles at arm's length and kept radio and television out of their homes. The group that had accepted telephones—and later cars—retained the original Wisler Mennonite name, while the Martin group became associated with the Old Order label.

In the late 1940s the Old Order Mennonites again suffered a division when a bishop and about one third of the members left to join the car-driving Wisler group. Meanwhile the Old Order Mennonite congregations in Ohio and Michigan had dwindled, reducing the Midwestern contingent of Old Orders to a relatively small group in Elkhart County. Since 1950, however, the Old Order Mennonites in northern Indiana have grown slowly but steadily in numbers, and in 1975 they constructed a third meetinghouse to accommodate their increased Elkhart County members.[3] A 1981 controversy that resulted in the silencing of a key leader has not dampened Old Order Mennonite growth.

Family and Community Life

Along with church, the family is central to Old Order Mennonite life. Informal education takes place in the home, where children absorb the disposition of *Gelassenheit* (submission) and practice the pattern of life prescribed by the community

Table 9.2. Most Common Indiana Old Order Mennonite Family Names

	% of households
Martin	40
Ramer	21
Imhoff	13
Weaver	7
Zimmerman	7
Burkholder	3
Shirk	3

Source: Old Order Mennonite Families, 2000: Indiana and Michigan (n.p., 2000).

and guided by church discipline. They learn gender roles by observing their parents' interaction. Only very rarely will an aging Old Order Mennonite person live in a nursing home. Most often grandparents live with or very near grown children and grandchildren, making the daily routines of home life multigenerational and intergenerational.

In addition to the generational overlap within households, there is a broader network of relationships tying family, church, and settlement together. Extended kin networks link most people within the settlement. Relatives populate the Sunday morning church service, the parochial school, and the business contacts that structure much of daily life. Several surnames dominate the settlement (see table 9.2). Some, like Martin and Ramer, are longstanding Indiana Old Order Mennonite names, whereas others, such as Fox and Nolt, represent relative newcomers to Indiana from Old Order settlements in other states. Nuclear families are large by modern standards, with an average of 8.25 children per household. Half the population is age eighteen or younger.

Like other Old Order groups, the Old Order Mennonites see education beyond the eighth grade as both a threat to stable community life and an unnecessary source of individual distinction and pride. Like the Old Order Amish, the Old Order Mennonites attended public schools until a combination of curriculum changes and school consolidation made them question the value of participating in that system. In 1969 they joined other conservative Mennonite and Brethren groups in starting a parochial school in the Yellow Creek area. As enrollment increased and more children withdrew from the public schools, each of the cooperating churches opened its own school.

Today all Old Order Mennonite students in the Elkhart County settlement attend one of five private schools operated by their church. Taught by Old Order Mennonite teachers who themselves are graduates of eighth-grade programs, the schools are one or two rooms in size with several grades in each classroom. The schools are similar to Amish schools in curriculum, approach to teaching, and parental involvement. While schools are conducted in English, the Old Order Mennonites' first language remains Pennsylvania Dutch. The important conversations of home and church are carried out in the dialect, as are most work and business encounters between members.[4]

The nature of Old Order Mennonite work has shifted in recent years even as it has remained largely home-centered. Traditionally, farming was the focus of Old Order labor. While some Old Order Mennonites worked in carpentry or skilled trades such as plumbing, most households engaged in small-scale farming, which in the 1900s often meant dairying. By the

Elkhart County's Old Order Mennonites were instrumental in establishing this wholesale produce auction near Wakarusa. The successful enterprise has helped keep family farming economically viable. Almost half of Indiana's Old Order Mennonites are still engaged in farming.
PHOTO BY DOTTIE KAUFFMANN.

late twentieth century, however, the agricultural economy had changed, encouraging some farm families to move into produce and other new cash crops. Old Order Mennonites were heavily involved in the 1994 establishment of a wholesale produce auction near Wakarusa that allows local farmers to obtain better prices for their products and keep family farming viable. (In fact, some Amish in nearby LaGrange County later began an auction modeled on the Old Order Mennonite success.)

Nevertheless, economic pressures have also pushed some Old Order Mennonites into nonfarm jobs. In addition, their growing population and the general lack of available farmland in Elkhart County has made the practical possibility of farming more difficult. Unlike many northern Indiana Amish who have opted for factory work as an occupational alternative, the Old Order Mennonites take a dim view of industrial employment. Today only a tiny number of married men work in the many factories that ring the Wakarusa, Goshen, and Nappanee communities surrounding the historic Yellow Creek settlement. Church leaders cite the unpleasant social environment of industry and the constant rubbing shoulders with "the world," along with the desire to keep work family-centered, as reasons against factory work.

Instead, Old Order Mennonites have established home-based small businesses such as welding shops, cabinet and furniture making, sawmills, and small machine shops. Others are involved in mobile work crews doing carpentry, roofing, or silo construction. Some families combine farming and a small sideline business as a way of keeping the family busy. It is not uncommon for younger unmarried or newly married men to work for fellow church members as a prelude to setting up their own businesses. Women operate some retail stores, especially fabric and dry goods stores.

In 2000 some 45 percent of Old Order Mennonite families in the Elkhart County settlement were engaged primarily in farming. Nearly the same percentage of household heads worked in small businesses, and 11 percent were employed in construction trades.

When population growth and a desire to remain in farming produced pressure on available land in the heart of the old Yellow Creek community, families explored new settlement possibilities in Indiana and neighboring states. In 1992 two new

Old Order Mennonite daughter settlements began, one near Tippecanoe, Indiana, and another near Carson City, Michigan. Not surprisingly, the percentage of farmers in the daughter settlements is higher than in the original Elkhart County community where land prices and suburban pressures are greater. In Tippecanoe, some 85 percent of households are farming.

One Tippecanoe resident reported that younger families tended to choose that community because it was closer to Yellow Creek and the extended family support they need when starting up a new farming operation. More established households, in contrast, tended to opt for the more distant Michigan location. In either case, church leaders warned against too much "running back and forth" between the settlements with the aid of hired cars or vans. While Old Order Mennonites may contract drivers for essential trips, they believe that—in the words of one member—"there is a certain amount of inconsistent light" when hiring drivers fosters unnecessary travel.

Although residents in these daughter settlements initially held church services and conducted school in their homes, they soon built meetinghouses and school buildings. Members living in different settlements remain connected through family ties and friendships. In addition, the settlements are formally linked through the Old Order Mennonite church conference. Although each of the daughter settlements has resident ministers, the Elkhart County Old Order Mennonite bishop serves both the churches in that area and the daughter settlements.

Church and Community Life

The church, of course, is what gives Old Order Mennonite people their identity. They have a deep appreciation for the

One of three Elkhart County Old Order Mennonite meetinghouses, this building reflects the simplicity and traditional values that mark Old Order Mennonite worship and church life. PHOTO BY THOMAS J. MEYERS.

past and see themselves in continuity with the New Testament church, the Anabaptist martyrs, and the early Mennonite immigrants to North America. When they gather for worship on Sunday mornings, they continue patterns of ritual that date to the early nineteenth century, if not earlier.[5]

Old Order Mennonites do not have geographic church districts like the Amish. Instead, all the members of the Elkhart settlement constitute a single church even though they do not all meet together in one place or at one time. Sunday services rotate among the three meetinghouses, with worship in two of the three on any given Sunday. Families attend whichever of the two services is closest to them.[6] The smaller Tippecanoe daughter settlement has only one meetinghouse and holds services there weekly.

In Indiana the Old Order Mennonite meetinghouses have a distinctive long pulpit behind which all the ordained men—bishop, ministers, and deacon—sit during the worship service. Other attendees do not sit as nuclear families, but rather as a corporate church family grouped by age and gender. Older men sit together, for example, as do older women, younger women, and younger men. Very small children sit with a parent.

The elements of Old Order Mennonite worship are similar to those of the Amish, though the order and details are somewhat different (see table 9.3). Nearly two hours long, services include a shorter opening sermon and a longer main sermon (often an hour in length) after which all ordained men present offer short "testimonies" to the truth and value of what was preached. Typically the congregation sings both a German and an English hymn. There is scripture reading and prayer—both silent and read from a prayer book—prayed by a kneeling congregation that physically assumes a humbled position.

An important feature of Old Order Mennonite church life is the semiannual church conference. In this regard the Mennonites differ significantly from the congregationally organized Amish. Even Amish church districts that find unity in a common Ordnung are functionally independent and self-governing. The Old Order Mennonites, by contrast, hold conferences that bring together leaders from various settlements to deliberate on matters of common concern. While the Old Order Mennonites in the Midwest once constituted their own conference, since 1973 they have been part of the Groffdale Conference—an Old Order Mennonite group centered in Pennsylvania but with membership in nine states.[7]

Church discipline and decisions about acceptable lifestyle practice are discussed at the spring and fall conference gatherings of Old Order Mennonite leaders. All of the members of

Table 9.3. Comparison of Old Order Amish and Old Order Mennonite Worship Services

Old Order Mennonite	Old Order Amish
Gather in gender and age groups	Gather in gender and age groups
Enter and sit in gender and age groups	Enter and sit in gender and age groups
Opening hymn	Opening hymn
Ministers enter	Ministers leave to prepare for service
Second hymn (lined by minister)	Ministers return/continued hymn singing
Opening sermon	Ministers return/opening sermon
Kneel for silent prayer	Kneel for silent prayer
Deacon reads scripture	Stand as minister reads scripture
Main sermon	Main sermon
Comments from other ministers	Testimony given by older men
Main speaker responds	
Kneel for audible prayer	Kneel for prayer read from prayer book
Benediction	Benediction
Closing hymn (lined by minister)	Closing hymn
Announcements	Announcements/matters of church business
	Fellowship meal

the conference adhere to the same discipline, so it is somewhat easier to generalize about Old Order Mennonite practice than it is about the Amish, whose congregational polity produces greater variety.[8]

In an important sense the Ordnung, or discipline, of the Old Order Mennonites is more formal than that of the Amish.

Like the Amish, Old Order Mennonites typically have large families.
All ages share in the work of the farm or the family's small business.
PHOTO BY DOTTIE KAUFFMANN.

The conference meetings discuss specific issues raised by ministers or bishops from any part of the conference and make
decisions for the entire body. The Groffdale Conference discipline—unlike that of most Amish settlements—is a written
document. All leaders and members of the conference are in
fellowship with one another and pledge to uphold conference
standards.

Like its Amish counterpart, the Old Order Mennonite discipline changes in ways that are slow and deliberate, not hap-
hazardly or individually fickle. For example, the conference has

long permitted tractor farming, but only with steel-wheeled tractors. Such a self-imposed restriction keeps the tractor a farm implement and not an alternative to the automobile, since steel-wheeled vehicles cannot be driven regularly on public roads. Even with tractors, many Old Order Mennonite farmers have continued also to use horse-drawn equipment, believing that both sources of power are useful in their own ways. Old Order Mennonite homes are wired for public utility electricity, though conference discipline limits the uses to which such power can be put. Television, radio, and computers (especially Internet access) are off limits. Old Order Mennonite families may subscribe to the local newspaper, but worldly broadcast entertainment is taboo.

Examples of more recent changes in Old Order Mennonite discipline are public utility electricity use and telephone ownership. Both were forbidden until 1973 when utility power was sanctioned for all members and lay households were permitted to obtain in-home phones. As an example and testimony against the necessity of phones, however, church leaders initially continued to forego telephone hookups. Since 1994 the conference has allowed leaders to have phones too.

Old Order Similarities and Differences

In their similarities and differences the Old Order Mennonites and Old Order Amish provide an illuminating example of what it means to be old order in a modern, changing world. Both groups have an old order worldview: they respect and value tradition; they do not assume that whatever is new is improved; they encourage yielding to church, community, family, and God instead of demanding individual fulfillment;

they interact with the government as subjects who receive privileges, not as citizens with civic rights and responsibilities; and they see the church as their primary community and view themselves as apart from, rather than a part of, larger society.

In a number of practical ways the Old Order Mennonites and Old Order Amish cooperate with one another. Some Old Order Mennonites subscribe to and write for Amish-published magazines such as *Family Life* and *Blackboard Bulletin*. Members of both groups work together on matters relating to parochial schools, share some curriculum materials, and attend joint meetings for parochial school teachers. Furthermore, the practical implications of maintaining a horse culture in an automobile-dominated society entail that members of both Old Order fellowships often frequent the same harness shops and horse auctions.

Yet there are significant differences between the two groups, at least as they exist in northern Indiana.[9] Observers note that the Mennonite refusal to work in industry and their greater commitment to small-scale farming has meant that there is less cash wealth in their community than among the Amish, resulting in fewer vacation trips or meals in restaurants and in somewhat more modest homes. The smaller size of the Mennonite community and the more unified conference discipline means that change tends to occur more slowly among the Old Order Mennonites and that settlement-wide standards are possible. Moreover, Amish young people in the region tend to engage in a wider range of social activities—within and beyond the bounds of the Ordnung—than do Old Order Mennonite teens.

Old Order Mennonites are somewhat more self-conscious about separation from worldly society and self-reflective in why they live as they do. The Old Order Mennonites live among a larger population of more progressive Mennonites who claim a similar denominational label but who live quite differently from the Old Orders. The Old Order Amish, in contrast, constitute the vast majority of people who go by the name Amish; in a sense, they define the Amish tradition as Old Order. The Old Order Mennonites do not have that public luxury and must consider their choices and changes more carefully relative to their mainstream Mennonite neighbors. In order to avoid confusion about their unique identity, they generally do not participate in events such as the progressive Mennonites' annual auctions to raise money for world hunger. Since the Amish are less threatened by association with Mennonites, they have been willing to be players in these progressive Mennonite charity projects.

In either case, both groups—Amish and Old Order Mennonite—live with a certain self-conscious confidence in the midst of a contemporary world, committed to being a people of God in spite of the costs and the difficulties that such a calling carries.

the world, and film documentaries have focused on teenage deviants from Indiana Amish homes.[1]

This newfound notoriety stems from several sources, including the Amish move into commercial and industrial occupations, where they increasingly rub shoulders with the wider world, and the urbanization and suburbanization that brings ever more non-Amish neighbors into traditional Amish settlements and establishes new arenas of interaction.

But if the added attention is easy to explain, the reasons behind the Amish appeal go deeper and speak as much to the needs of modernity as to the strengths of the Old Order. At its heart, the attraction flows from Old Order values themselves, which increasingly stand in contrast to modern American society. In a world bemused by progress and continually promising itself that the best days lie just ahead, a people who anchor their identity in old authorities—the Bible, tradition, memories of European persecution—are a curiosity. In a society that celebrates the individual and glories personal achievement, those who call for submission to the community and defer to Ordnung are noteworthy. In a larger culture that prizes self-sufficiency, the practice of mutual aid stands out as remarkable. Moderns are fascinated by the living presence of such values and commitments even when they do not fully understand them. The Old Order example of communities that witness to a different reality has never been more prominent than it is today.

Yet notoriety has its costs, not the least of which is the temptation to generalize, to sentimentalize, and to judge from afar all Amish by the actions of a few. Unlike the two-dimensional logos often used to hawk Amish wares, Amish society itself is more like a richly colored, multi-textured patchwork quilt, with pieces of different sizes, histories, and colors.

Their communities are composed of real people with their own interests, habits, and inclinations. Their settlements are vibrant in large part because they are not uniform or frozen in time but are dynamic communities closely connected to local lives.

Just as the quilt maker creates a pattern with many different quilt pieces, enduring Old Order beliefs and values stitch together an Amish patchwork from various histories, habits, customs, and cultures, producing a pattern precisely because the pieces are different. Commitment and conviction do not extinguish contingency or context. Community and tradition have a way of joining together differences and diversity. For moderns who believe there might be warmth and comfort in the Old Order patchwork quilt, that insight may be the most important to ponder.

Notes

INTRODUCTION

1. "Officials Cut Ribbon on Nonmotorized Roadway," *Goshen News*, 22 November 2002, A-1.

I. THE OLD ORDERS

1. Reporters, scholars, and Old Order people themselves have defined the term "Old Order" in a number of different, if related, ways. Several key discussions include Beulah Stauffer Hostetler, "The Formation of the Old Orders," *Mennonite Quarterly Review* 66 (January 1991): 5–25; Donald B. Kraybill and Carl F. Bowman, *On the Backroad to Heaven: Old Order Hutterites, Mennonites, Amish, and Brethren* (Baltimore: Johns Hopkins University Press, 2001), 1–19; and Theron F. Schlabach, *Peace, Faith, Nation: Mennonites and Amish in Nineteenth-century America* (Scottdale, Pa.: Herald Press, 1988), 201–29. For the purposes of this book, we have defined the term in a simple and pragmatic way: Old Orders are those churches whose members use horse-and-buggy transportation on the road. While this definition does not get at the essential heart of Old Order life and values, it is a handy way to delineate who we are including. In fact, many Amish writers and historians use this working definition in their own writing.

2. Nearly 180,000 Amish can be found in twenty-eight U.S. states and the Canadian province of Ontario. The most accurate current statistics are available in David Luthy, "Amish Settlements Across America: 2003," *Family Life*, October 2003, 17–23. *Family Life* is a monthly magazine issued by the Amish-owned Pathway Publishers of Aylmer, Ontario. Other recent statistics may be found in Donald B. Kraybill, *The Riddle of Amish Culture*, rev. ed. (Baltimore: Johns

Hopkins University Press, 2001), appendix C. The population of Old Order Mennonites is approximately 24,000; see Kraybill and Bowman, *Backroad to Heaven*, 67.

3. Kraybill, *Riddle of Amish Culture*, rev. ed., 33.

4. The emphasis on *Gelassenheit* as a key ingredient of the Amish worldview has been succinctly expressed in the work of Donald Kraybill (see Kraybill, *Riddle*, rev. ed., 29–32).

5. *Martyrs' Mirror* was originally issued in 1660 in Dutch. The German version, kept in print by the Amish, is Thieleman J. van Braght, *Der blutige Schauplatz, oder, Märtyrer-Spiegel der Taufgesinnten, oder, Wehrlosen Christen . . .* (Aylmer, Ont.: Pathway Publishers, 1996). The English edition, kept in print by a Mennonite press, is Thieleman J. van Braght, *The Bloody Theatre, or Martyrs Mirror of the Defenseless Christians . . .* (Scottdale, Pa.: Herald Press, 1998).

6. *Ausbund: das ist, Etliche schöne Christliche Lieder* (Lancaster, Pa.: Verlag von den Amischen Gemeinden in Lancaster County, Pa., 1997). For more information on this hymnal and the Amish understanding of the theology its hymns reflect, see the Amish-authored volume Benuel S. Blank, *The Amazing Story of the Ausbund* (Narvon, Pa.: the author, 2001). About half of the *Ausbund* song texts are translated into English in *Songs of the Ausbund*, vol. 1: *History and Translations of Ausbund Hymns* (Millersburg, Ohio: Ohio Amish Library, 1998).

7. Data drawn from Jerry E. Miller, comp., *Indiana Amish Directory: Elkhart, LaGrange, and Noble Counties, 2002* (Middlebury, Ind.: the compiler, 2002). Obviously, the most current data on the size and composition of the Amish population is constantly changing. Unless otherwise noted, data in this book comes from the most recently published settlement directories. Typically, such Amish church directories are updated and reissued every seven to ten years.

2. MOVING TO INDIANA

1. These stories are chronicled in David Luthy, *The Amish in America: Settlements That Failed, 1840–1960* (Aylmer, Ont.: Pathway Publishers, 1985); and David Luthy, *Why Some Amish Communities Fail: Extinct Settlements, 1961–1999* (Aylmer, Ont.: Pathway Publishers, 2000).

2. Surveys of the Anabaptist movement include J. Denny Weaver, *Becoming Anabaptist: The Origin and Significance of Sixteenth-century Anabaptism* (Scottdale, Pa.: Herald Press, 1987); and C. Arnold Snyder, *Anabaptist History and Theology: An Introduction* (Kitchener, Ont.: Pandora Press, 1995).

3. Documentation and interpretation of this schism is found in John D. Roth, trans. and ed., *Letters of the Amish Division: A Sourcebook* (Goshen, Ind.: Mennonite Historical Society, 1993).

4. Mennonite immigration began in 1683 but involved only a handful of households until 1707; thereafter, Mennonite immigration was steady through the 1770s.

5. A survey of European and North American Amish history is available in Steven M. Nolt, *A History of the Amish,* rev. ed. (Intercourse, Pa.: Good Books, 2003).

6. From a narrative by John E. Borntreger (1837–1930), son of one of the land scouts, published as *Geschichte der ersten Ansiedelung der Amischen Mennoniten* (Elkhart, Ind.: Mennonite Publishing Co., 1917), and in English as *A History of the First Settlers of the Amish. . . .* trans. Elizabeth Gingerich (Topeka, Ind.: Dan A. Hochstetler, 1988), 5.

7. Evidence uncovered by David L. Habegger suggests that the first Amish man to settle in Adams County arrived in 1840, a decade earlier than the 1850 date that previously had been assumed and that was often reported in historical chronologies. See David L. Habegger and Karen C. Adams, *The Swiss of Adams and Wells Counties, Indiana 1838–1862* (Fort Wayne, Ind.: D. L. Habegger, 2002), 44–67.

8. Information on Indiana settlements comes from fieldwork and interviews carried out by Thomas J. Meyers and Steven M. Nolt in each community; some dates and data on non-Indiana settlements comes from Luthy, "Amish Settlements Across America: 2003."

9. There are locally published histories of some Amish settlements; among them is Joseph Stoll, *The Amish in Daviess County, Indiana* ([Aylmer, Ont.: Joseph Stoll], 1997).

10. In fall 2003 a family from the Elkhart-LaGrange settlement in northern Indiana moved to Switzerland County in the southeast corner of the state, hoping to begin a new settlement. If enough other households join them, they will become the twentieth—and newest—Amish community in Indiana. There is already one Amish set-

tlement in Switzerland County, but this new migration venture—
should it prove successful—would constitute a distinct settlement
because it has a different origin and affiliation from that of Switzerland County's older, ethnically Swiss Amish settlement.

11. Bontrager's life is detailed in Eli J. Bontrager, *My Life Story*
([Goshen, Ind.: Manasseh E. Bontreger], 1982).

3. MAINTAINING THE OLD ORDER

1. In a few cases settlements established in recent years have
prepared a written Ordnung covering some—though not all—aspects
of church discipline. This approach is helpful in those places where a
new settlement is composed of households migrating from different
places (each with its own Ordnung) and that may be unfamiliar with
one another's expectations and assumptions. In such cases, a written
Ordnung replaces the orally transmitted and generally understood
Ordnung that existed in those older communities.

2. The Indiana meetings were held in 1864 in Elkhart County
and in 1872 in LaGrange County. For a more detailed history of
those meetings and mid-nineteenth-century Amish life, see Paton
Yoder, *Tradition and Transition: Amish Mennonites and Old Order
Amish, 1800–1900* (Scottdale, Pa.: Herald Press, 1991). Yoder intro-
duced the terms "tradition-minded" and "change-minded" to describe these groups. The minutes of the gatherings are available in
English as Paton Yoder and Steven R. Estes, *Proceedings of the Amish
Ministers' Meetings, 1862–1878* (Goshen, Ind.: Mennonite Historical Society, 1999).

3. In recent years several subgroups have formed within the
Swartzentruber affiliation, but these events have not divided the Indiana settlement. The so-called "Nebraska Amish" of central Pennsylvania is the only other affiliation that is more traditional in its
lifestyle and outlook than the Swartzentrubers. There are no "Nebraska Amish" in Indiana.

4. The New Order Amish did not choose the New Order designation and initially resisted it as not representative of their efforts
to reform (rather than reject) tradition. For a time the New Order
Amish used the term "Amish Brotherhood" to describe themselves,
but most eventually accepted the New Order Amish name since it

quickly became the widespread label for their group. There are two different subgroups within the New Order circle of churches; both districts in Indiana associate with the group that has the slightly more conservative Ordnung. In addition, since 1986 in Ohio there has been a small group known as the New Order Fellowship, which might be considered the most progressive of affiliations. That group has no members in Indiana. For a concise overview of New Order origins and theology written by two New Order Amish leaders, see Edward A. Kline and Monroe L. Beachy, "History and Dynamics of the New Order Amish of Holmes County, Ohio," *Old Order Notes* 18 (Fall–Winter 1998): 7–19.

5. Statistics in this book and most other sources offering national or state population figures for the Old Order Amish include the New Order groups under the Old Order heading, allowing horse-and-buggy use to mark a rough but practical definition of who is Old Order.

6. For a sympathetic history, see Elmer S. Yoder, *The Beachy Amish Mennonite Fellowship Churches* (Hartville, Ohio: Diakonia Ministries, 1987).

7. Steven M. Nolt, "The Amish 'Mission Movement' and the Reformulation of Amish Identity in the Twentieth Century," *Mennonite Quarterly Review* 75 (January 2001): 7–36, explains some of these developments and their impact on the Old Orders.

4. AMISH ETHNICITY

1. Amish of Pennsylvania Dutch ethnic extraction rarely identify themselves as Pennsylvania Dutch—though they will identify their spoken dialect with that name. However, they do use the term "Swiss" to refer to members of that Amish ethnic group and to the dialect spoken by that group.

2. On Pennsylvania Dutch as it is spoken in Indiana, see Steve Hartman Keiser, "A Different Kind of Deitsch: The Origins and Development of Midwestern Pennsylvania German," Ph.D. diss., Ohio State University, 2001.

3. Chad L. Thompson, "The Languages of the Amish of Allen County, Indiana: Multilingualism and Convergence," *Anthropological Linguistics* 36 (1994): 69–91, argues that the Swiss dialect in Allen

County is actually an Alsatian dialect—a contention some linguists debate. Swiss Mennonite immigrants settled in Ohio about the same time as the Swiss Amish moved to Indiana. A detailed study of the Swiss dialect spoken in all of these places is Marion R. Wenger, "A Swiss-German Dialect Study: Three Linguistic Islands in Midwestern U.S.A.," Ph.D. diss., Ohio State University, 1969.

4. Swiss families who move to Pennsylvania Dutch-speaking settlements may retain a Swiss accent, but they soon switch to the prevailing dialect. Pennsylvania Dutch speakers who move to Swiss communities, in contrast, often retain their Pennsylvania Dutch dialect much longer.

5. This designation of the non-Amish as "English" is typical everywhere except in Geauga County, Ohio, and related Amish settlements, where the Amish term for outsiders is "Yankees."

6. Although some linguists have developed grammars and spelling systems for Pennsylvania Dutch, the Amish have not adopted these.

7. Although this newspaper has a German name, it is written in English. The founders of the paper hoped that giving it a German title would cause most "English" people to ignore it.

8. It is not uncommon for Amish people to also own and read English Bibles (King James Version) or German-English parallel translations.

9. These matters are governed by local church Ordnung, not ethnicity itself. Nevertheless, many of the traditions prescribed in the Ordnung express ethnic custom. Some of the especially tradition-minded Amish settlements of Pennsylvania Dutch extraction (such as the Swartzentruber Amish and the Paoli, Indiana, settlement) are actually more conservative in lifestyle than are most of the Swiss.

10. Chad L. Thompson, "Yodeling of the Indiana Swiss Amish," *Anthropological Linguistics* 38 (1996): 495–520.

11. Among the Swiss Amish, the symbolic social avoidance of the excommunicated (shunning) is a lifelong condition unless and until the excommunicated person confesses error and returns to the church. The Amish refer to this practice as *streng Meidung* (strong shunning). *Streng Meidung* is also the practice of some Pennsylvania Dutch–speaking Amish groups—notably the Lancaster, Pennsylvania, settlement and the so-called Swartzentruber and Andy Weaver

Amish in Ohio and related settlements. However, in Indiana the majority of Amish of Pennsylvania Dutch background do not practice *streng Meidung*. While excommunication and shunning in these settings are very real, shunning may be lifted without a formal confession on the part of the errant former member. If an excommunicated person eventually shows him- or herself to be a faithful member of a related Anabaptist group, the Amish may "lift the ban" and end the practice of symbolic social avoidance.

5. COMMUNITY AND FAMILY LIFE

1. The only Amish settlement in Indiana with a church meetinghouse is the New Order community near Salem.

2. The Amish in the Daviess County settlement and the Salem New Order church district do not use the *Ausbund*, but use variations of it. The Daviess County Amish sing from the *Unparteiische Liedersammlung*, and the Salem church uses a variation of this Daviess County book. Both of these books include the "Loblied," and the Amish in these places also sing it as the second hymn.

3. While the Amish hold both the biblical Old and New Testaments as authoritative, and sermons draw illustrations and insights from all portions of Scripture, the texts that are read in worship and that form the basis of Amish preaching come exclusively from the New Testament, mostly from the Gospels (Matthew, Mark, Luke, and John) with their accounts of the life and teaching of Jesus. This focus is important for understanding Amish theology. See John S. Oyer, "Is There an Amish Theology?" in *Les Amish: Origine et Particularismes, 1693–1993*, ed. Lydie Hege and Christoph Wiebe (Ingersheim: Association Française d'Histoire Anabaptiste-Mennonite, 1994), 278–302.

4. The small Amish community in Sarasota, Florida, is the only truly urban settlement in North America. That community is very unusual because its residents are mostly elderly people who spend their winters in Florida to escape the harsher climates in Indiana, Ohio, and Pennsylvania.

5. This community is also unique because many of these families live in contemporary log homes that are clustered on a hillside overlooking a riverbed.

6. Traditionally, weddings were held on Tuesdays or Thursdays. Today, in the large Elkhart-LaGrange and Nappanee settlements where many household heads work in factories through the week, weddings sometimes take place on Saturdays so that attendees will not have to take a day off work, suggesting one way that new work patterns have encouraged an Amish adaptation to North American notions of the "weekend" (a segment of time that was not so distinct in traditional agrarian life). In these settlements weddings are held any day of the week but Sunday or Monday. Weddings require a great deal of work the day before, so a Monday wedding is not possible, given Amish commitments to refraining from any unnecessary work on Sunday.

7. It is not possible to give comprehensive data on family size for every settlement in the state because not every community produces a settlement directory. In addition, the newer settlements are disproportionately comprised of younger families with women in their childbearing years; thus, it is impossible to determine with confidence the average size of completed families in these settlements.

8. In 2002 the documentary film *The Devil's Playground* (Wellspring Media Inc.) featured the stories of four Amish teens and young adults from the Elkhart-LaGrange settlement engaged in highly deviant (and sometimes illegal) behavior. The film, which also aired on cable television, was embarrassing to the Amish community and prompted some church leaders to admonish parents to try to maintain greater oversight of their children's activities. The stories presented in the film were authentic, although they presented a less-than-typical slice of Amish life. To cite but two examples: all four characters had attended public school and only one (or 25 percent) ended up joining the Amish church. In fact, a solid majority of children in the Elkhart-LaGrange settlement attend Amish parochial schools, and more than 90 percent join the church in young adulthood.

9. In January 2004 UPN Studio announced plans for an Amish-theme "reality television" series on Amish teen life. Among the many erroneous assumptions behind the concept of the program was one related to the point made here: Amish teens are not ignorant of the wider world, but if and when they engage it, they do so in particularly Amish ways, not in the mode of typical American teenagers, even when their activities seemingly parallel those of mainstream teens.

10. For a detailed analysis of the factors that affect the decision for or against church membership, see Thomas J. Meyers, "The Old Order Amish: To Remain in the Faith or to Leave," *Mennonite Quarterly Review* 68 (July 1994): 378–95.

11. The Swiss Amish also do not bury in family plots, but simply bury individuals in the order in which they die.

12. It should be noted that the sorts of changes described here are not widespread in the most conservative settlements. Women's lives in such places continue to revolve much more around food preservation and traditional household tasks with very few laborsaving devices and only rare outlets for independent entrepreneurial business ventures.

13. See concerns expressed in the Amish-published magazine *Family Life*, including "The Future of Farming," October 1993, 28–34, and "The Family Farm Is Alive," June 1994, 25–30.

14. Suzanne M. Bianchi and Lynne M. Casper, "American Families," *Population Bulletin* 55 (December 2000): 4. It should be noted that many single households in America include individuals who were formerly married and now live alone after a divorce. Divorce is virtually nonexistent among the Amish, and thus the Amish single households are almost exclusively individuals who have never married.

15. Data derived from Owen E. Borkholder, comp., *Nappanee Amish Directory, including the Rochester, Kokomo, and Milroy Communities, 2001* (Nappanee, Ind.: compiler, 2001).

6. AMISH SCHOOLS

1. Dorothy Ann Overstreet Pratt has carefully documented the details of these early school cases in her dissertation, "A Study in Cultural Persistence: The Amish in LaGrange County, Indiana, 1841–1945," Ph.D. diss., University of Notre Dame, 1997.

2. Nearly a decade earlier, Amish men had been arrested in Geauga County, Ohio, when their children had not attended high school. See Albert N. Keim, *Compulsory Education and the Amish: The Right Not to Be Modern* (Boston: Beacon Press, 1975), and Thomas J. Meyers "Education and Schooling," in *The Amish and the State*, 2nd. ed., ed. Donald B. Kraybill (Baltimore: Johns Hopkins University

Press, 2003), 87–106, for an overview of the history of Amish conflicts with state and local governments over school matters.

3. Luthy, *Amish in America: Settlements That Failed,* 109.

4. This time the court showed leniency, merely levying a $25 fine, and the Amish agreed to hire a certified non-Amish woman as their teacher (ibid.). The matter of whether Amish parents had the right to establish their own schools continued to be controversial in many places. The issue was finally settled by the important U.S. Supreme Court decision *Wisconsin v. Yoder.* On May 15, 1972, the Court unanimously ruled that the Amish are not required to send their children to high school. For a full transcript of the case, see Keim, *Compulsory Education,* 149–81.

5. Pratt, "Study in Cultural Persistence," 171. This concern over the financial impact of lower enrollments in public schools as a result of Amish children attending parochial schools continued throughout the twentieth century. Occasionally local school administrators have tried to entice Amish parents to send their children to public schools for only a few hours per week in order to boost enrollments and secure dollars from Indianapolis. See John Zehr, "Allen County, Indiana School Movement," *The Diary,* January 1998, 67–68, for a description of such an attempt in Allen County.

6. The traditional Amish position is that human faces should not be reproduced. This would be a violation of the biblical commandment against graven images and may also exalt the individual whose image is being reproduced and thus lead to pride.

7. Joseph Stoll, *Who Shall Educate Our Children?* (Aylmer, Ont.: Pathway Publishers, 1965), 26, 31.

8. Among the first cases of consolidation that affected the Amish were those near the city of Dover, Delaware, in the 1920s and in Lancaster County, Pennsylvania, in the 1930s. See Meyers, "Education and Schooling."

9. The school in Nappanee was the Borkholder School; in LaGrange County, Pleasant Ridge School; and in Allen County, Amish School #1.

10. See Meyers, "Education and Schooling," for more detail about this decision.

11. Details of the development of the school committee and negotiations with the state were taken from an interview with David

Schwartz on November 11, 1999. Superintendent Wells is still held in high esteem among the Amish and considered a public servant who was able to balance the requirements of the state with the needs of particular constituents.

12. Most Amish schoolteachers are technically self-employed. Thus the school has no obligation to pay Social Security benefits. The Amish do not participate in the Social Security program or other social welfare programs. For a description of their objections to these programs and the history of the legal process that led to an official exemption from Social Security in 1965, see Peter J. Ferrara, "Social Security and Taxes," in *Amish and the State*, 2nd ed., ed. Kraybill, 125–43.

13. Very occasionally an Amish school board will hire a non-Amish teacher. (Co-author Meyers was such a teacher during the 1981–82 school year.) For more detailed descriptions of the role of the Amish schoolteacher, see Andrea Fishman, *Amish Literacy: What and How It Means* (Portsmouth, N.H.: Heinemann, 1988); and John A. Hostetler and Gertrude Enders Huntington, *Amish Children: Education in the Family, School, and Community*, 2nd ed. (New York: Harcourt Brace and Jovanovich, 1992).

14. *Regulations and Guidelines for Amish Parochial Schools of Indiana* (Middlebury, Ind.), 5.

15. Hostetler and Huntington, *Amish Children*, 94.

16. Thomas J. Meyers, "Old Order Amish: To Remain in the Faith or to Leave," *Mennonite Quarterly Review* 68 (July 1994): esp. 380, 392–94.

17. The teacher with the most seniority in this school also carries the title of principal, which is quite unusual for an Amish school.

18. *Blackboard Bulletin*, December 2002, 13–14.

19. For a brief description of special education in Nappanee, see Borkholder, comp., *Nappanee Amish Directory*, 49.

7. AMISH WORK

1. Donald B. Kraybill and Steven M. Nolt, *Amish Enterprise: From Plows to Profits*, 2nd. ed. (Baltimore: Johns Hopkins University Press, 2004), esp. chap. 14.

2. Jean Seguy, "The Vocational Life of the French Anabaptists

from the Seventeenth to the Nineteenth Centuries," *Mennonite Quarterly Review* 67 (July 1973): 182.

3. Walter M. Kollmorgen, *Culture of a Contemporary Community: The Old Order Amish of Lancaster County, Pennsylvania,* Rural Life Studies No. 4 (Washington, D.C.: U.S. Department of Agriculture, 1942), 20.

4. For an example of agricultural experimentation in North America, see Grant M. Stoltzfus's description of Pennsylvania Amish farmer David Mast's creative use of ground bone to replenish the nutrients of the soil and increase his yield of oats: "History of the First Amish Mennonite Communities in America," *Mennonite Quarterly Review* 28 (October 1954): 235–62.

5. Thomas J. Meyers, "Lunch Pails and Factories," in *The Amish Struggle with Modernity,* ed. Donald B. Kraybill and Marc A. Olshan (Hanover, N.H.: University Press of New England, 1994), 165–81.

6. The minor exception to this general statement is the few Adams County men who work in factories near Decatur. In most other Old Order communities, factory work is either unavailable or industry labor is unionized. The Amish church forbids participation in organized labor, citing its confrontational tactics as contrary to the nonresistant life and cautioning against joining any worldly organizations.

7. Data calculated from Jerry E. Miller, comp., *Indiana Amish Directory: Elkhart, LaGrange, and Noble Counties, 1995* (Middlebury, Ind.: J. E. Miller, 1995).

8. "Minutes of Bruderhand Meeting," August 25, 1998, 5.

9. In the most tradition-minded settlements, including the communities near Paoli and in Steuben County, the church does not permit such "mixed partnerships," and the use of power tools, even when owned by others, is discouraged or forbidden.

10. For a discussion of the significance of agriculture for the survival of Amish society, see Eugene P. Erickson, Julia A. Erickson, and John A. Hostetler, "The Cultivation of the Soil as a Moral Directive: Population Growth, Family Ties, and the Maintenance of Community among Old Order Amish," *Rural Sociology* 45 (Spring 1980): 49–68; and William H. Martineau and Rhonda Sayres MacQueen, "Occupational Differentiation among the Old Order Amish," *Rural Sociology* 42 (1977): 383–97.

11. Thomas J. Meyers has argued that factory work has, in fact, made it possible for some Amish men to remain Amish; see "Old Order Amish: To Remain in the Faith or to Leave," 378–95.

8. THE AMISH AND THEIR NEIGHBORS

1. Although since the middle of the twentieth century most Amish have become increasingly integrated into the economic affairs of larger society, the Amish parochial school movement that blossomed during the same era has in its own way fostered an increase in Amish cultural separation from mainstream society. Thus, while many Amish now work and shop in ways that often mirror their non-Amish neighbors, their social lives, friendship networks, and core cultural values are perhaps more distinct than ever, and many Amish children are socialized more completely into the Amish world than were their grandparents.

2. This is changing with more Amish products being marketed via the Internet by non-Amish entrepreneurs. Non-Amish persons have developed websites advertising Amish products. Many Amish business people are also beginning to use answering services that allow them to maintain some distance from phone communication but do permit indirect contact with customers.

3. Data are for 1998; see Elkhart and LaGrange data in *Economic Impact of Elkhart County's Tourism and Travel Industry–1998* (Lexington, Ky.: Certec, Inc., 1998). Although tourism is an important industry in Indiana, it has not reached the proportion of the tourist activity in Holmes County, Ohio, or Lancaster, Pennsylvania. Donald Kraybill suggests that each year there are 180 visitors per Amish person in Lancaster County, and these visitors spend $1.2 billion dollars and generate about $177 million in tax revenue (*Riddle of Amish Culture*, rev. ed., 287).

4. *Amish Country Northern Indiana* (2003), 3; *Amish Country Northern Indiana* (2001), 31.

5. *Amish Country Northern Indiana* (2001), 24.

6. See the 2000 survey research and analysis in Thomas J. Meyers, "Amish Tourism: 'Visiting Shipshewana Is Better than Going to the Mall,'" *Mennonite Quarterly Review* 77 (January 2003): 109–126.

7. Kraybill, *Riddle of Amish Culture*, rev. ed., 293.

8. Ibid.

9. See, for example, the Associated Press story "New Mental Health Clinic Tailored to Amish Values" that appeared in various newspapers on 14 February 2002.

10. Limb-girdle muscular dystrophy is particularly prevalent in the Adams County settlement. For a summary of this research, see Victor A. McKusick, "Forty Years of Medical Genetics," *Journal of the American Medical Association* 261 (1989): 3155–58.

11. New Eden was developed on the model of the very successful Mount Eaton Care Center serving the Amish in Wayne County, Ohio, since 1985; see Gertrude Enders Huntington, "Health Care," in *Amish and the State*, 2nd ed., ed. Kraybill, 174.

12. Ibid., 170–72. Both situations resulted in some compromise and out-of-court settlements.

13. In many of the newest settlements in the state, the Amish have been warmly welcomed because of the skills and services they bring to a community. They may introduce furniture businesses for the local market or provide blacksmithing and harness shops.

14. The implications of such licensing varies, with some counties requiring an annual fee and others a one-time registration charge; some counties insist that buggies bear license plates, while others require only a license document to be kept in the buggy. The diversity of requirements is particularly noticeable in the Nappanee settlement that spans four counties, not all of which have the same regulations. Some buggies in the Nappanee settlement have license plates, others do not.

15. David Wagler, "Not Afraid of Persecution," *Family Life*, July 1970, 10.

16. Members of the Swartzentruber Amish affiliation have received some national notoriety for resisting the use of bright orange SMV emblems on their buggies but have not had any conflicts over the matter in Indiana. By the time the Swartzentruber Amish first began moving to Indiana in 1994, the state had agreed to recognize as an alternative the use of reflective silver tape, which the Swartzentrubers found less offensive than the SMV emblem. For wider context, see Lee J. Zook, "Slow-moving Vehicles" in *Amish and the State*, 2nd ed., ed. Kraybill, 145–60.

17. *Goshen News*, 16 November 1990, A-5.

18. *Lancaster New Era,* 18 February 1995, B-14.

19. For more information on this agreement, see Marc A. Olshan, "Homespun Bureaucracy: A Case Study in Organizational Evolution," in *Amish Struggle with Modernity,* ed. Kraybill and Olshan, 199–213.

9. A DIFFERENT PART OF THE PATCHWORK

1. There is a third, very small horse-and-buggy-driving group in Indiana in addition to the Amish and Mennonites. The Old Brethren German Baptist Church near Camden in Carroll County, Indiana, has about fifty adherents and exists only in Indiana. Historically and doctrinally, it is related to the Brethren movement originating in 1708 in Schwarzenau, Germany, that combined Anabaptist and Pietist religious streams. The Old Brethren German Baptists may be considered the Old Order relative of the culturally mainstream Church of the Brethren denomination. A related and larger (5,000-member) car-driving group of Old German Baptist Brethren are also often considered an Old Order fellowship within the Brethren family of churches but do not fit our definition of horse-and-buggy-driving Old Orders. For information on these car-driving Old German Baptist Brethren, see Kraybill and Bowman, *On the Backroad to Heaven,* 137–78. There are very few printed sources on the small group of horse-driving Old Brethren German Baptists.

2. Quoted in Theron F. Schlabach, *Peace, Faith, Nation: Mennonites and Amish in Nineteenth-century America* (Scottdale, Pa.: Herald Press, 1988), 224.

3. Old Order Mennonites in Elkhart-St. Joseph Counties had had three meetinghouses until the 1950s when one was closed due to membership losses. By 1975 the church again needed three meetinghouses.

4. A significant exception is the Old Order Mennonites in Virginia. Virginia Mennonites had already switched to English language conversation and worship before the 1901 division that produced the Old Order body. Thus, the Old Order group there has always been English speaking—a fact that Old Order Mennonites in other states often point out.

5. Documents detailing church practices and rituals from the

early nineteenth century and a comparison with certain current Old Order Mennonite practices are found in David J. Rempel Smucker, ed., and Noah G. Good, trans., "Church Practices of Lancaster Mennonites: Writings by Christian Nissley (1777–1831)," *Pennsylvania Mennonite Heritage* 13 (July 1990): 2–11. Documentation of church practice and worship from the eighteenth century is uneven and thus difficult to generalize and compare.

6. Since 1981 a small Elkhart County Old Order Mennonite group under the leadership of bishop William G. Weaver uses the third meetinghouse in rotation with the larger Groffdale group's use of the other two.

7. There are three horse-and-buggy Old Order Mennonite conferences: Groffdale Conference, Ontario "Woolwich" (Old Order) Conference, and Virginia "Cline" (Old Order) Conference. The Groffdale Conference is the largest, and the Virginia group the smallest. In addition there are a number of very small, loosely affiliated Old Order Mennonite churches with roots in these three conferences. For more on the Groffdale Conference Old Order Mennonites, see Kraybill and Bowman, *On the Backroad to Heaven*, 60–100; and Stephen E. Scott, *An Introduction to Old Order and Conservative Mennonite Groups* (Intercourse, Pa.: Good Books, 1996), 28–69. Both books focus on the Groffdale Conference churches in Pennsylvania, so some details and history do not apply to the Indiana Groffdale church.

8. There is a notable exception to this pattern, however. Since the Indiana Old Order Mennonites had a separate conference history prior to joining the Pennsylvania-based Groffdale Conference in 1973, their discipline was different from the Groffdale patterns and practices in a few specifics. As part of their process of uniting, the Indiana churches (and their subsequent daughter settlements) retained their traditions but agreed to submit to all conference decisions made after 1973.

9. From 1995 to 1999 there was a small Old Order Mennonite settlement near Salem in southern Indiana's Washington County near several Washington and Orange County Amish communities. The Salem Old Order Mennonites were a daughter settlement from the Virginia Old Order Mennonite conference. The settlement did not attract many members, and eventually the pioneer households returned to Virginia. During their brief existence in Indiana these

Mennonites had some contact with the neighboring Amish, participating in barn raisings and several other community functions, but contact was limited.

AFTERWORD

1. The so-called "Electric Amish," originating in Indianapolis and led by Dean Metcalf (a.k.a. Graber Goodman), perform such parodies. The widely distributed 2002 film *The Devil's Playground* was shot in Elkhart and LaGrange Counties. On the Electric Amish, see David Weaver-Zercher, *The Amish in the American Imagination* (Baltimore: Johns Hopkins University Press, 2001), 5–7. Weaver-Zercher's book is a cogent presentation of how and why American popular culture seemingly venerates Amish culture while ultimately dismissing it as hypocritical or unrealistic (what Weaver-Zercher calls the dual "saving remnant" and "fallen people" motifs).

For Further Reading

AMISH HISTORY AND LIFE

Hostetler, John A. *Amish Society.* 4th ed. Baltimore: Johns Hopkins University Press, 1993. Comprehensive discussion of many aspects of Amish life.

Hostetler, John A., and Gertrude Enders Huntington. *Amish Children: Education in the Family, School, and Community.* 2nd ed. New York: Harcourt, Brace, Jovanovich, 1992. Description of Amish schools, curriculum, teachers, and the socialization of Amish children.

Kraybill, Donald B. *The Riddle of Amish Culture.* Rev. ed. Baltimore: Johns Hopkins University Press, 2001. Readable book that explores the logic of Old Order life through the lens of the Lancaster, Pennsylvania, Amish community.

Kraybill, Donald B., ed. *The Amish and the State.* 2nd ed. Baltimore: Johns Hopkins University Press, 2003. Chapters on conflicts involving public schools, Social Security, military, health care systems, local government, and other matters.

Kraybill, Donald B., and Steven M. Nolt. *Amish Enterprise: From Plows to Profits.* 2nd. ed. Baltimore: Johns Hopkins University Press, 2004. Charts the shift away from farming, with focus on the Lancaster, Pennsylvania, Amish; also has a chapter on Midwest Amish employment patterns.

Kraybill, Donald B., and Marc A. Olshan, eds. *The Amish Struggle with Modernity.* Hanover, N.H.: University Press of New England, 1994. Essays on a range of topics illustrating cultural change.

Nolt, Steven M. *A History of the Amish.* Rev. ed. Intercourse, Pa.: Good Books, 2003. Three-century survey of Amish history in Europe and North America.

Stoltzfus, Louise. *Amish Women: Lives and Stories*. Intercourse, Pa.: Good Books, 1994. Stories of nine Amish women and reflections by the author who grew up in an Amish family.

OLD ORDER MENNONITE HISTORY AND LIFE

Horst, Isaac R. *Separate and Peculiar: Old Order Mennonite Life in Ontario*. 2nd ed. Waterloo, Ont.: Herald Press, 2001. Explanation of Old Order Mennonite life and beliefs by a Canadian Old Order church member.

Kraybill, Donald B., and Carl F. Bowman. *On the Backroad to Heaven: Old Order Hutterites, Mennonites, Amish, and Brethren*. Baltimore: Johns Hopkins University Press, 2001. Comparison of four Old Order groups, including the Old Order Mennonites of Lancaster, Pennsylvania.

Scott, Stephen E. *An Introduction to Old Order and Conservative Mennonite Groups*. Intercourse, Pa.: Good Books, 1996. Basic information about Old Order Mennonites across North America.

PUBLICATIONS BY AMISH AND OLD ORDER MENNONITE AUTHORS

Pathway Publishers (Aylmer, Ontario, and LaGrange, Indiana) is an Old Order Amish publisher whose books and magazines are also read by many Old Order Mennonites. Some Old Order Mennonites also write for Pathway. To receive a Pathway catalogue, write to Pathway Publishers, 2580 N 250 W, LaGrange, IN 46761.

In addition to books for adults and children, Pathway issues three periodicals. *Family Life* is their monthly magazine of stories, nonfiction articles, children's features, and editorials; *Young Companion* provides reading material for youth and young adults; and *Blackboard Bulletin* is a magazine for Amish schoolteachers and children. Sample copies or subscriptions are available by writing to the address above.

Index

industrial, 114–117; Old Order Mennonites, 150–153; small businesses, 49, 117–121, 130–131; and social change, 116–117, 121–122; women, 87–88

Ohio: Belle Center, 38; Bellefontaine, 52; Canton, 69; Holmes County, 31, 52, 177n3; Mount Hope, 137; Tuscarawas County, 31; Wayne County, 38, 147–148

Old Brethren German Baptists, 179n1

Old German Baptist Brethren, 179n1

Old Order, defined, 4–5, 43, 143, 165n1

Old Order belief system, 5–17

Old Order Mennonites, 3–4, 21; church buildings, 154–155; church discipline, 147, 155–158; compared with Amish, 158–160; daughter settlements, 152–153, 180n9; family, 148–150; history, 143–148; horse drawn transportation, *144, 145;* occupations, 150–153; Ordnung and conference organization, 145, 155–158; schools, 150; telephone and automobiles, 148, 153, 158; typical surnames, 149; worship services, 153–156

Ontario, 34, 147, 165n2

Orange County, Ind., 37, 50, 111, 128

Ordnung, 13, 33–34, 41–50, 55–56, 156, 168n1

Painview School, *94*

Paoli, Ind., 37, 127, 137

Paoli Amish settlement, 7, *12,* 37, 50–51, 137–138, 170n9, 176n9

Paoli Swartzentruber Amish settlement, 7, 37, 50, 170n9, 176n9

Parke County, Ind., 111

Parke County Amish settlement, 7, 35–37, 47–48, 102, 109–112, 131

Pennsylvania, 31, 33, 47; Lancaster County, 30, 35–37, 103, 110–111, 131, 137, 140, 170n11, 177n3; Mifflin County, 30; Somerset County, 30

Pennsylvania Dutch (Pennsylvania Deitsch) dialect, 3, 60–62, 145

Pennsylvania Dutch Amish ethnicity, 58–68

"Pennsylvania Dutch Country," 127

Pennsylvania German dialect. *See* Pennsylvania Dutch

Population: Indiana Amish, 4, 166n7; North America Amish, 165n2

Protestant Reformation, 21, 24

Reformed Church, 30, 69

Reist, Hans, 27, 29

THOMAS J. MEYERS is Professor of Sociology and Director of International Education at Goshen College. He has studied Amish society for more than twenty years and has published numerous articles and book chapters on Amish life.

STEVEN M. NOLT is Associate Professor of History at Goshen College. He is author of *A History of the Amish*, rev. ed. (2003) and (with Donald B. Kraybill) *Amish Enterprise: From Plows to Profits*, 2nd ed. (2004).